TO

FROM

OCCASION

THE
Daniel
CODE

Living Out Truth
in a Culture That Is
Losing Its Way

O. S. Hawkins

COUNTRYMAN®
A Division of Thomas Nelson Publishers

THOMAS NELSON
Since 1798

Published in Nashville, Tennessee, by Thomas Nelson. Thomas Nelson is a registered trademark of HarperCollins Christian Publishing, Inc.

Cover design by Left Coast Design, Portland, Oregon. www.lcoast.com

Thomas Nelson titles may be purchased in bulk for educational, business, fund-raising, or sales promotional use. For information, please e-mail SpecialMarkets@ThomasNelson.com.

978-0-7180-8994-8

Printed in China

24 25 26 WAI 7 6 5

THE
Daniel
CODE

Living Out Truth
in a Culture That Is
Losing Its Way

O. S. Hawkins

*I love the words of Daniel 1:21, which say,
"Thus Daniel continued . . ."*

The Daniel Code *is dedicated to all those faithful
servants who* continued *to minister with dedication
and determination in those out-of-the-way places where
they often wondered if they had been forgotten. They
lived on meager pastors' salaries with little extra to put
aside for their declining years. Since all the author's
royalties and proceeds from* The Daniel Code *go to
support them, you have had a part in being Christ's
hand extended by purchasing this book. Mission:
Dignity is here to enable these faithful pastors, their
wives, and their widows to live out their final years with
the kind of security and dignity they so richly deserve.*

TABLE OF CONTENTS

INTRODUCTION

Culture Shock

s I type the words *culture shock*, my mind is racing back over the decades of my life. Flashing before me are the many changes I have personally witnessed in the cultural collapse of the Judeo-Christian ethic of our Western world in my lifetime.

I was born in 1947 and spent my boyhood days in the 1950s, when tens of thousands of American troops had just returned home from Europe and the South Pacific at the conclusion of World War II. They married their high school sweethearts, and what sociologists have termed the baby boom began. In the 1950s, we were a grateful and thankful people. Average church attendance was at an all-time high. We never locked our doors at night. I left my bicycle in the front yard every evening, and it was always still there the next morning. We heard Bible readings each morning over the intercoms of our public elementary schools. The Ten Commandments were prominently displayed on the class-room walls, and once a year some good and godly folks called the Gideons visited our school and gave every student a copy of the New Testament. As always happens, the mood of the culture was reflected in the music of the day. Doris Day had one of the biggest hit songs of the era in "Que Sera, Sera (Whatever Will Be, Will Be)." It was a new day of optimism and hope.

Change Is in the Wind

Then came the 1960s. I have always felt a bit sorry for those folks who didn't get to spend their teenage years in the golden oldie days of the '60s—the days of madras Windbreakers, Bass Weejun shoes, glasspack mufflers, and sock hops. But in sharp contrast were certain events that did something to the psyche of our nation: the assassination of President John F. Kennedy in 1963 and our entrance into the Vietnam War. At the same time, Dr. Martin Luther King was rallying the righteous with his nonviolent civil disobedience efforts exposing the nation's long and ugly sins of racial hatred and segregation. His own assassination in Memphis left a wound that has not been fully healed to this day. We shifted from the more innocent and optimistic white-picket-fence mentality of the '50s to one that became extremely introspective. Once again the culture was reflected in the music. Peter, Paul and Mary had one of the biggest hits of that decade when they sang, "The answer, my friend, is blowing in the wind." Many Americans realized that the answers they thought they had were simply blowing in the wind. The culture became immersed in introspection.

Next came the 1970s, the decade of such traumatic events as Watergate and the resignation of a president, the legalization of abortion in *Roe v. Wade*, and ongoing involvement in Vietnam. I watched as the culture moved from one that was introspective to one that became extremely skeptical. Skepticism influenced the mind-set of millions, and it showed up in the music. Billy Joel, the piano man, had one of the biggest hit songs of the '70s when he sang, "Only the good die young." Skepticism in a nutshell.

Then came the 1980s, and Ronald Reagan spoke of the United States as that "shining city on a hill." The economy grew, and new hope permeated the fabric of our national pride. Then we saw the Berlin Wall come crashing down on the other side of the Atlantic, an international event that fueled hope in our nation

In the 1990s, the USSR—the "evil empire"—collapsed, and the Cold War came to an end. This was followed by the start of a new millennium, and a horrific event in the first decade of the twenty-first century scarred the psyche of our nation. The infamous 9/11 attack on America changed profoundly the way we think and go about our everyday lives.

AND HERE WE ARE TODAY . . .

So my own grandchildren are growing up today in a culture where issues that slithered down the darkened back alleys of my childhood now parade themselves proudly down the main streets of every city and town in America. We have watched an entire culture slowly but surely sink into a moral malaise of unfathomable proportions. How can we believers and our faith in Jesus survive in our modern, counter-Christian-cultural world?

We aren't the first followers of God to face this situation. The Old Testament hero Daniel wrote the book on how God's people can survive in a pagan, permissive, and perverted culture. He was born in Jerusalem and grew up there until he was taken captive to Babylon as a young man. He found himself uprooted from a Jewish culture built upon the Mosaic moral law and dropped into one that was foreign to everything he had known and been taught. Daniel could have spent his energy blaming his circumstances on societal ills, the court system of his day, government policies, political leaders, or the educational system, just as we Christians in our contemporary culture can place blame today. However, Daniel steps off the pages of Scripture and into our modern culture to reveal some principles, a sort of "Daniel Code," that can enable us not to simply survive in our culture but to engage it, thrive in it, and even be used by the Lord to transform it.

A Believer's Options

Can we really expect to change a culture that is crumbling around us? I absolutely believe so, but it is interesting to observe the various ways in which people of faith address the culture today. There are those who *compromise*: they accept cultural ideas—including the call to tolerance—that subtly shift their allegiance away from following Christ and Him only. Some believers *condone* the culture around them: they find it simply much easier to adapt to a changing culture and accept alternative lifestyles. Others *condemn*: they beat their Bibles a little harder and scream a little louder. But, thank God, there are some believers who—like Daniel—choose to *confront* the culture and engage it by speaking truth in love.

I am not minimizing how hard that last option is. After all, we have evolved into a schizophrenic society. We listen as ministers pray at presidential inaugurations and then punish high schoolers who try to pray at football games or valedictorians who attempt to insert a prayer in graduation speeches. We cry out for law and order in the streets and, at the same time, teach kids in our classrooms that there are no moral absolutes. And we wonder why relativism runs rampant in our society! And the list goes on. While crying out to stop the rapid rise of illegitimate births, we at the same time allow the government to continue to subsidize the type of behavior that guarantees its rise. We are concerned about the high rate of teens involved in sex, but instead of emphasizing abstinence, we provide them free condoms in public schools. We speak of the dire need to keep families together while we liberalize divorce laws so that it becomes easier and easier to simply walk away. And on . . . and on . . . and on.

And this is the culture we, as believers, are called and commissioned to engage and reach. Not many years ago, one's failures and perversions were occasions of shame or at least embarrassment. This is not true in our postmodern world: what were once considered perversions are now occasions for public promotion and stardom on television talk shows. And too many of us believers remain hunkered down behind stained glass walls, opting to isolate and shelter ourselves from the world outside. Some of us continue to live as if we were in a world governed by an ethic and culture that is compatible with the truth of the Bible—but we aren't. Besides, Christ has called upon us to be salt and light in this dying and dark world (Matthew 5:13–16).

A Biblical Example

In the book of Acts, the early church exploded when Paul and other believers stepped out of their comfort zones and engaged a culture completely different from the one they had known. Likewise, God calls us to engage a culture that is not the least bit interested in our stained glass or our morals. It is a culture that is not only asking, "Is the Bible true?" They also want to know, "Is it relevant?" Does this Book written in an ancient Middle Eastern culture hundreds of years ago have any relevance in a world where we are transplanting organs, experimenting with genetic engineering, and sending probes to the farthest reaches of our solar system? And they will never know the answer to those questions—and the answer is "Absolutely yes!"—unless we engage them.

This is where Daniel comes in. He has been there. He has done that. And he had amazing success, as we will see as these pages unfold before us. Let's begin unlocking the Daniel Code. Let's listen carefully to him . . . and learn from him.

SECTION I
THE REMOTE CONTROL SYNDROME

*M*y wife, Susie, and I have spent decades in a beautiful marriage. We seldom, if ever, disagree on major decisions, and verbal arguments and conflicts are rare around our house. However, such was not the case on a recent evening.

At the center of our little spat was that oblong black gadget we call the television remote control. We were lying in bed, and Susie was trying to go to sleep. I was happily engaged with my remote control, moving from news stations to sports stations and back and forth, surfing the channels with abandon. All of a sudden, "faster than a speeding bullet and more powerful than a locomotive," Susie sat upright, reached over, and grabbed the remote right out of my hand! Guess what? I didn't like that one bit. Why? Its name explains it: remote *control*. We like to stay in control of things around us. It was not a good feeling to find myself suddenly out of control of even the TV. Similarly, holding tight to the (imagined) controls of the circumstances of life swirling around us gives us a sense of security. There is just something about each of us that wants to stay in control.

The book of Daniel, written more than twenty-six hundred years ago, is the story of a young man who suddenly found himself in a situation in which he had no control. He was removed from his comfort zone. Overnight, he had been taken from all he had known in his Jewish culture in Israel, carried off as a captive, and plopped into the middle of the foreign pagan culture of Babylon. The remote control had been jerked right out of his hand.

When we hear the name *Daniel*, some may think, *Old Testament* and picture a long-bearded, out-of-date old prophet, an old guy with no idea what it would be like to live in our crumbling culture in a postmodern Western world with all of its struggles and challenges. But Daniel was a real young man, wholesome and handsome, living in a real world and facing real problems just as you and I do. He had a real job in a real marketplace. In that workplace he was surrounded by real men and women who were hostile to his belief system and its values. They held to their own New Age approach to life. His bosses were real—and they were backstabbing and vain. They were constantly taking credit for others' work as they tried to get ahead.

Clearly, Daniel would have felt right at home in our modern, secular environment. So this Daniel definitely has something to say to us about finding our own way in a culture that has lost its way. He has a lot to say to us . . . including some dos and don'ts for not simply surviving in a world hostile to our faith, but also for succeeding and truly engaging it to make a long-term difference. He speaks from experiential knowledge, having been there and done that very thing.

Help ... and Hope

With every passing week our own culture sees a greater stripping away of religious liberties that have been held dear since the founding of our nation. Political correctness long ago replaced personal convictions in the halls of our palaces of power. We will go out again this week to live out in our own modern, pagan culture what we say we believe. Young people will go to school, where they will be confronted with values and belief systems that their grandparents would not have believed. We awake every day to a world of standards and principles, statutes and provisions that are foreign to most everything the Bible teaches.

Daniel's story is the story of a young man who can well understand our own challenges. This is the story of a young man who confronted the same kind of difficult decisions that we are called upon to make every day. He was dropped into a culture that was forcing him to stuff all his religious roots and convictions back into the corner of his workplace closet. His world tempted him to take the easy route to the top and go along with the crowd. Yet Daniel's influence still lives across these centuries as an inspiration to all of us who clash with our culture every day in our own postmodern world. His is a story of help ... and hope.

Three Timeless Truths

So what advice does Daniel have for us today? He has three basic things to say. Put these three statements in bold block letters in the PowerPoint of your mind.

- *Don't Give In. Be Resistant.* Our general tendency—and the far easier route—is to simply give in to the culture and go its way. Now, Daniel did in fact give in to some nonessentials, like language and literature, but he drew the line on certain other things, like diet and prayer. He had to make some tough decisions, and he did not compromise. He didn't isolate himself from the culture around him, but he did insulate himself from it. He drew the line where issues became contrary to certain scriptural principles he believed and held dear.

- *Don't Give Up. Be Consistent.* If we do not stay on guard, we tend to simply give up when we become overwhelmed by cultural pressures seeking to fit us into its mold. Daniel never gave up, even when the temptation to ask, "What's the use?" must have been great. He stayed consistent not only in what he believed but in how he behaved.

- *Don't Give Out. Be Persistent.* As I noted in the dedication, I love the words recorded in Daniel 1:21, "Thus Daniel continued." He was committed to God for the long haul . . . and, as we shall see, he finished strong. He was persistent, and he won in the end. His influence on an entire nation made an indelible and incredible difference. His words for us are not simply theoretical: they were tested in places of great difficulty, like a den of lions, for example.

Daniel knows what you are up against when you leave home in the morning to enter the marketplace. He knows exactly what you are facing when you pack your backpack and leave for school to face the incredible peer pressure of political correctness. Daniel has walked where you are walking today. He has a lot to say to any and all of us who feel as if the remote control of life has been jerked from our grasp. He begins with a caution not to give in. Turn the page and give him a hearing.

1   DON'T GIVE IN: BE RESISTANT

Part 1

In the third year of the reign of Jehoiakim king of Judah, Nebuchadnezzar king of Babylon came to Jerusalem and besieged it. And the Lord gave Jehoiakim king of Judah into his hand, with some of the articles of the house of God, which he carried into the land of Shinar to the house of his god; and he brought the articles into the treasure house of his god.

Then the king instructed Ashpenaz, the master of his eunuchs, to bring some of the children of Israel and some of the king's descendants and some of the nobles, young men in whom there was no blemish, but good-looking, gifted in all wisdom, possessing knowledge and quick to understand, who had ability to serve in the king's palace, and whom they might teach the language and literature of the Chaldeans. And the king appointed for them a daily provision of the king's delicacies and of the wine which he drank, and three years of training for them, so that at the end of that time they might serve before the king. Now from among those of the sons of Judah were Daniel, Hananiah, Mishael, and Azariah. To them the chief of the eunuchs gave names: he gave Daniel the name Belteshazzar; to Hananiah, Shadrach; to Mishael, Meshach; and to Azariah, Abed-Nego.

But Daniel purposed in his heart that he would not defile himself with the portion of the king's delicacies, nor with the wine which he drank; therefore he requested of the chief of the eunuchs that he might not defile himself.

—DANIEL 1:1–8

*D*aniel was keenly aware of the temptation to yield to the pressures of the culture around him. After all, he was a long way from home and who would really know if he, for instance, changed his diet? Yet he chose to resist the pressures and not to give in to them. He drew the line. Note, however, that he went along with some things, nonessentials like learning the language or reading Babylon's history. But Daniel resisted at each and every point he was called upon to do something that was diametrically opposed to his convictions regarding God's commands. Daniel made some really tough decisions when many around him found it easier to go along and give in. To fully understand the significance of what is happening, we need to ask ourselves some questions: *where, who, when, what,* and *why*.

Where does this all take place? Daniel's story begins at home in Judah. After the reign of King Solomon, the twelve tribes of Israel divided into ten tribes in the north and two in the south. The northern kingdom never had one good king and met its end in 722 BC when they were taken away into Assyrian captivity. In the south, over three and a half centuries, nineteen kings ruled from its capital in Jerusalem.

While many of the kings strayed from their biblical convictions, several of them were good kings. It was here in the southern kingdom of Judah that Daniel was born, and we meet him when he was a teenager. The other place mentioned is Babylon, located in modern-day Iraq. In Daniel's day, Babylon had become the antithesis to everything Bible believers hold dear. It was the heart of paganism and the undisputed world power of its day.

A better understanding comes with a knowledge of *who* was on center stage in Daniel's story. There was Nebuchadnezzar, the king of Babylon. He was an electrifying leader who built an incredible city and developed a world empire. Next, we meet Jehoiakim, king of Judah, on his throne in Jerusalem. Sadly, he was nothing more than a spineless puppet. He led the Jews to worship other gods and "did evil in the sight of the LORD" (2 Kings 24:19). The Bible places the blame squarely on him for filling Jerusalem "with innocent blood" (v. 4).

We are also introduced to a young man by the name of Daniel, who was a descendant of good King Hezekiah. As a boy, he was caught up in the spiritual revival under King Josiah, an experience that had a profound impact on his young life. Extremely bright and handsome, if he lived in our modern world, he would no doubt be elected as "Most Likely to Succeed" at any school he attended. But his world, with all its promise, was turned upside down when the Babylonians conquered Jerusalem and took him captive back to Babylon.

So *when* did all this take place? Daniel 1:1 reveals that

these events ensued during the "third year of the reign of Jehoiakim." That would date this episode in 605 BC. By God's design, these were days of severe punishment and persecution of God's straying people. Nebuchadnezzar rounded up a small group of the brightest and most promising young people of Judah and carried them back to Babylon. When the destruction of Jerusalem became complete in 587 BC, Daniel had already been in exile throughout his teen years and into his early adulthood.

Finally, *what* was actually taking place? It was nothing short of the judgment of God Himself. The Bible frames it by saying, "The Lord gave Jehoiakim king of Judah into [Nebuchadnezzar's] hand" (Daniel 1:2). God was in control, and the lesson is . . . He still is in control. He is holding the remote. He is pushing the buttons. In a real sense, this wicked king of Babylon was nothing more than the remote control in the hand of God. Jeremiah even quoted the Lord as calling Nebuchadnezzar "My servant" (Jeremiah 25:9).

Not a lot of people in our modern world seem to believe that God still judges sin and that He actually still holds in His hand the remote control over our lives and all history. For years, this coming Babylonian captivity had been predicted by God's prophets in amazing detail (Isaiah 39:5–7; Jeremiah 25:8–12; 2 Kings 20:17–18). However, Judah would not repent. Warning after warning came their way, but they blindly believed they were indestructible. Before we are too quick to point a finger of accusation their way, we should examine ourselves to see if we are not sailing the seas of uncertainty in the same boat.

Once the people of Judah were taken away into captivity, we only have to read Psalm 137:1–6 to catch a glimpse into their hearts:

By the rivers of Babylon
> *There we sat down, yea, we wept*
> *When we remembered Zion.*
> *We hung our harps*
> *Upon the willows in the midst of it.*
> *For there those who carried us away captive asked of*
> > *us a song,*
> *And those who plundered us requested mirth,*
> *Saying, "Sing us one of the songs of Zion!"*

How shall we sing the LORD's song
> *In a foreign land?*
> *If I forget you, O Jerusalem,*
> *Let my right hand forget its skill!*
> *If I do not remember you,*
> *Let my tongue cling to the roof of my mouth—*
> *If I do not exalt Jerusalem*
> *Above my chief joy.*

Yes, it was the Lord who gave the Jews into Babylonian captivity.

And *why* did God allow this? After all, He once called Israel the "apple of His eye" (Zechariah 2:8), but the Bible says, "Whom the Lord loves He chastens" (Hebrews 12:6). The captivity was not designed so much to scourge His people as to purge them. Many good things resulted in the aftermath. Israel never again followed after idols, and that remains true to this very day. The Hebrew Bible began to come together under men like Ezra. The remnant of God's people eventually returned to Jerusalem, and in it was the seed of our Messiah. This captivity carried God's message of hope and love to heathen lands. A few centuries later, when the Magi came from this same region to Bethlehem to worship the Christ child, it was because their forefathers had heard of Him from Daniel and passed the account down through the generations. And all this happened because Daniel refused to give in: he stood resistant to the pressures around him. He stood for what he believed. We need many more like Daniel today.

2 DON'T GIVE IN: BE RESISTANT

Part 2

*A*n interesting plot is unfolding in the story of Daniel and his young Hebrew friends who found themselves captives in this foreign land . . .

Nebuchadnezzar had conceived an ingenious plan. He was among the first to recognize something in the DNA of the Jewish people that has brought about a better world for all of us. What would our modern world be without the contributions of Einstein, Salk, Sabin, Freud, Disraeli, Singer, Pulitzer, and a multitude of others like them? Thus, Nebuchadnezzar's plan was to corral the brightest young Jewish minds, immerse them in his own Babylonian culture, reeducate them completely, and eventually send them back to Israel to rule there on behalf of Babylon. It was a clever plot, and these young Jewish exiles certainly had impressive résumés for that job. Daniel 1:4 lists their qualifications: "no blemish . . . good-looking, gifted in all wisdom, possessing knowledge and quick to understand, who had ability to serve." They were the sharpest of the sharp with the highest SAT scores and polished social graces. All Nebuchadnezzar had to do now was brainwash these monotheistic boys and transform them into polytheistic leaders.

So the stage was set. First, Nebuchadnezzar set out to change their *language*. His plan was to completely do away with Hebrew as a spoken language. And it worked. One of the miracles of the modern state of Israel is the revival of the ancient spoken language of the Jews. It lay dormant from the days of Nebuchadnezzar until 1948 when the state of Israel was established. Now when you walk the streets of Tel Aviv and Jerusalem, you hear Hebrew again after all these centuries. (If our current immigration issues have taught us anything, it is that to be fully accepted in any new culture, one must learn to speak its language.) So these young Hebrew lads were thrust into language school. Gone was the language of Zion for them.

Nebuchadnezzar next set out to change their *literature* (Daniel 1:4). Literature is, after all, the window through which most cultures can be viewed. The king sought to fill these bright young minds with Babylonian philosophy, science, astrology, and religion. His stated goal was to reeducate them away from the deep roots of their previous belief system with all its traditional values. This is still being done in our modern educational systems today: we call it "values clarification."

The king was not only intent upon changing the young captives' language and literature but also their *lifestyle*, starting with their diet (Daniel 1:5). He appointed rich provisions for them daily. These boys were given gourmet delights straight from the king's table. But remember, these were Jewish lads who had grown up on a strict kosher diet.

Nebuchadnezzar's intent here went far beyond the introduction of tasty new foods. Underneath all that was a sinister attempt to change their lifestyles. And Nebuchadnezzar was not finished yet.

THE FOREIGN CULTURE

Nebuchadnezzar wanted to change the boys' language, literature, and lifestyle, but his ultimate goal was to change their *loyalties*. He changed their names (Daniel 1:7). Daniel and his three young friends had Hebrew names that spoke about who they were and where they were from. The name *Daniel* literally means "God is my Judge." *Hananiah* means "beloved of the Lord." *Mishael*'s name meant "who is like God." *Azariah*'s name meant "the Lord is my help." Today we know these last three men far better by their Babylonian names, Shadrach, Meshach, and Abed-Nego, which refer to the pagan gods Bel and Aku rather than to Yahweh, as their Hebrew names did. By changing their names he was attempting to change their loyalties. Again, Nebuchadnezzar's long-term plan was to train these young leaders to handle all the affairs of the exiles in Babylon and then to eventually rule over them when they returned home to Jerusalem as fully indoctrinated Babylonians, thus enlarging the footprint of his kingdom.

We look upon this conniving approach with a bit of disdain, and yet the very same thing has been going on in our own culture for decades. Our brightest young minds are being reeducated according to principles that are foreign to those of all our Founding Fathers and foreign to our Christian faith. As far back as 1933, the Humanist Manifesto set out its plain objectives, but few people paid any attention and most scoffed it off. Its stated goal was to "bring young people to deny the deity of God and the biblical account of creation." It set out to "reeducate young people to the fact that moral values should be self-determined and situational." In other words, there is no absolute truth. This manifesto also stated the intent to remove distinctions between the roles of male and female in society. This didn't just happen in 2015 with the legalization of gay "marriage." It had been decades in the making. The Humanist Manifesto also advocated the right of abortion and euthanasia and argued vigorously for the redistribution of wealth in America. In many ways we have become the Babylon of the modern era. We apparently learned our lessons well at the feet of Nebuchadnezzar himself. It is little wonder that we have lived to see Bible reading eliminated from public schools, the Ten Commandments removed from public view, and creation science excluded from classroom instruction. None of this is new: this thinking has its roots in Babylon. Clearly, the book of Daniel is one of the most relevant books of the Bible for our world today.

A Strategy

Daniel walked the corridors of a crumbling culture that is much like ours, but he did not give in. He remained resistant. How? It wasn't because others were protesting or picketing or trying to elect new leaders. He remained resistant because early on, back in Jerusalem, he had been "trained in the way he should go" (Proverbs 22:6). He was well grounded in truth, and that truth had been rooted in him by his parents.

In our modern world we like to think it "takes a village" to raise our children. No, it takes a strong mom and dad to raise these precious young minds in the way in which they should go. When they are left to "the village," it will pull our kids down every time. Daniel may not have been able to control the cultural influences of Babylon swirling around him, but he still held the remote control when it came to how he would react to them. The Bible says he "purposed in his heart that he would not defile himself with the portion of the king's delicacies" (Daniel 1:8). Even though he was learning a new language and an accompanying new literature, Daniel drew the line when it came to eating the king's meat, an act contrary to his Hebrew faith. Daniel would not compromise when it came to the Word of God and His commands. Thus, the Bible simply says, Daniel "purposed in his heart" not to turn from his God.

It is of utmost importance to note that Daniel made no attempt to separate himself from the culture around him. He was no isolationist as some would advise we become today. Daniel was fully capable of interacting with the pagan culture around him but not be contaminated by it. An isolationist mentality leaves no place for believers to be salt and light as our Lord calls us to be (Matthew 5:13–16). We need what Daniel had: a knowledge of what is biblical and what is not as well as a commitment to the biblical. Part of our problem today is that, for too long, we have been in retreat. Some of us have given in to the world's ways while others have given up on even engaging the pagan culture around us.

We should identify with Daniel as much as, if not more than, we do with anyone on the pages of the Bible. Take a good look at him. He was under incredible pressure to conform to the culture, to just give in. Everything around him had changed. His language changed. What he was now reading was the complete antithesis to all he had studied before. Neither he nor his friends were even called by their real names any longer. He was being squeezed into the Babylonian mold. He fought hard against a determined effort to cut him off from all his religious roots.

As we look around our own world today, so much is the same. It is as though the remote control has been ripped from our own hands, and we, too, are tempted just to give in.

Consider for a minute what criteria, if any, you use to determine which activities in our own culture to engage in or not. Daniel relied on the Word of God for guidance. Daniel had set his mind, he had "purposed in his heart," and he had predetermined which way he was going to turn long before he got to the intersection. Life is filled with intersections, and compromise is key to getting along with our culture today. Sadly, compromise has too often become the American Christian's way. Daniel is shouting to us across the centuries, "Don't give in! Be resistant."

3   Don't Give Up: Be Consistent

But Daniel purposed in his heart that he would not defile himself with the portion of the king's delicacies, nor with the wine which he drank; therefore he requested of the chief of the eunuchs that he might not defile himself. Now God had brought Daniel into the favor and goodwill of the chief of the eunuchs. And the chief of the eunuchs said to Daniel, "I fear my lord the king, who has appointed your food and drink. For why should he see your faces looking worse than the young men who are your age? Then you would endanger my head before the king."

So Daniel said to the steward whom the chief of the eunuchs had set over Daniel, Hananiah, Mishael, and Azariah, "Please test your servants for ten days, and let them give us vegetables to eat and water to drink. Then let our appearance be examined before you, and the appearance of the young men who eat the portion of the king's delicacies; and as you see fit, so deal with your servants." So he consented with them in this matter, and tested them ten days.

And at the end of ten days their features appeared better and fatter in flesh than all the young men who ate the portion of the king's delicacies. Thus the steward took away their portion of delicacies and the wine that they were to drink, and gave them vegetables.

—DANIEL 1:8–16

*C*ultural collapses are like earthquakes: they don't just happen. They are both preceded by a series of seemingly insignificant cracks below the surface that converge and build until they eventually erupt, resulting in all kinds of devastation. Let's face it. When it comes to dealing with cultural and moral collapse, it is easier for some to simply give up on their convictions and principles and go along with the flow. If Daniel has anything to say to us across these generations, it is to never give up, to stay consistent, and to be true to the God we love. And Daniel practiced what he preached.

Daniel stated bluntly to the king's chief eunuch that he "would not defile himself" by partaking of the king's meat that was not kosher, no matter how delectable and delicious it looked (Daniel 1:8). Daniel wouldn't give in . . . or give up. He was determined, and eventually the Babylonian authorities "consented" to test and see if Daniel's diet would suffice (v. 14).

As this scene from Daniel's life illustrates, one key to success in life, no matter the circumstances, is this element of being consistent in what we say and how we act. We see its importance all through the Bible: Joseph was falsely accused and sat in an Egyptian dungeon, and Paul exercised civil disobedience and found himself in a Philippian jail cell. Just Like Daniel, they didn't give up. And God did not forget any of them. His hand was on the remote control.

Just Say No

Let's review. Daniel went along with the Babylonian teaching because he already knew what he believed. He went along with the name change because he knew they might change his name, but they could never change his heart. But Daniel drew the line when it came to eating the king's meat. Many of us, however, would think a different choice would make more sense. That is, we would go along with something as seemingly inconsequential as food but say no to the name change. Had Daniel asked me, I might have even counseled him to stay away from that pagan literature, not to pollute his mind with godless morals. So why did Daniel say yes to the education and no to the food? The answer is plain: Daniel drew his lines based on what the Word of God specifically said. There is no biblical prohibition against taking a different name or learning what others believe. However, there was a strong prohibition about what a Jew was to eat. Not only was Nebuchadnezzar's food not kosher, but it had been offered to idols. So Daniel didn't refuse to eat it because he was a vegetarian or some kind of dietary fanatic. Daniel chose to obey God's command. He took his stand upon the Word of God. He was consistency personified.

Taking a Stand

One reason so many professed believers falter and fail when confronted with our modern culture's values is that they simply do not know what the Bible says. So they compromise and assimilate themselves into the culture around them because they have little or no real heart convictions. Too seldom do we, like Daniel, "purpose in our hearts" so that when decision-making time comes, we have already made it in our minds and hearts.

In our modern world with so many vices too easily tolerated, many of us may ask, "Where is God?" He was there with Daniel. And He is still here with us. Remember, it was God Himself who gave Israel into Babylon's hand (Daniel 1:2). And this same God "brought Daniel into the favor and goodwill" of the Babylonian authorities (v. 9). God had not abandoned His throne . . . then or now. He is in total control.

When we establish and live by biblical standards as Daniel did, God has a way of showing up on our side. Daniel "purposed in his heart" (v. 8). He made his choice. He had set his mind to doing the right thing. God still holds the remote control in His hand. He can turn us up or turn us down. He can turn us on or turn us off. He can change our channel or mute us at His will as He desires.

We need to follow Daniel's example. We seem to think if we don't give up and just go along, we might not get that promotion, or we might even lose our position. Daniel knew who he wanted on his side, and it was not his boss. It was the living God. Daniel knew the truth of Proverbs 16:7, "When a man's ways please the LORD, He makes even his enemies to be at peace with him."

LIFE LESSONS

So what is the point? If we are going to get anywhere in life, there are some wise lessons to be learned from our friend Daniel. Don't play politics. Live aligned with the Word of God. Forget trying to be a people pleaser; your task is to please God. And it is not enough to simply resist the culture around us if we who are God's people are not consistent in what we say and how we act.

Finally, one of the most appealing aspects of Daniel's conduct was that he was not self-righteously trying to prove something to someone. This choice to not eat the king's food was no show. It was from his heart. Daniel had a disarming way about him that pleased God and ultimately gave him favor with those who sought to rule over him. We would all get further in life if we were as wise as Daniel was. Can you hear him right now? I don't think he is speaking softly in some kind of a whisper. I think he is shouting, "Don't give in! Be resistant! And don't give up! Be consistent!"

4   Don't Give Out: Be Persistent

As for these four young men, God gave them knowledge and skill in all literature and wisdom; and Daniel had understanding in all visions and dreams.

Now at the end of the days, when the king had said that they should be brought in, the chief of the eunuchs brought them in before Nebuchadnezzar. Then the king interviewed them, and among them all none was found like Daniel, Hananiah, Mishael, and Azariah; therefore they served before the king. And in all matters of wisdom and understanding about which the king examined them, he found them ten times better than all the magicians and astrologers who were in all his realm. Thus Daniel continued until the first year of King Cyrus.

—DANIEL 1:17–21

I love these words "Thus Daniel continued" (Daniel 1:21). Daniel finished strong! He was persistent. He outlived Nebuchadnezzar. He even outlived the entire once-supreme Babylonian empire. Daniel lived into the days of Cyrus, the ruler of the Medes and Persians, and God used Daniel to make a tremendous difference in his culture and his world.

USED BY GOD

Throughout the Bible we see that God has His own ways of watching over His own when they remain faithful to His Word and obedient to His will. It was of course God who brought Daniel into "favor and goodwill" with his captors (Daniel 1:9). It is a comfort to know in the midst of a crumbling culture that the Lord has the remote control in His hand. God also imparted to Daniel "knowledge and skill in all literature and wisdom" (v. 17). At the end of this initial three years, the time came for Daniel to take his oral exams. He flew through them at the head of the class. Preparing intellectually to address ideas and behaviors contrary to our faith is a requirement for living in our own Babylonian culture. Like Daniel, we no longer live in Jerusalem ourselves. In our Babylonian world, we are to tolerate heretical ideas and unbiblical behavior. Our culture seems to have an increasing disdain for anything related to the religious liberties we have cherished for 250 years. It is crucial for us, like Daniel, to live uncompromising lives; not to quit, not to give out . . . to be persistent in a culture where our cherished values stand in stark contrast to what it proclaims.

Daniel was indeed persistent. We read that "Daniel continued until the first year of King Cyrus" (Daniel 1:21), and that covered a time span of seventy years. Throughout all those decades, Daniel never gave in . . . never gave up . . . and never gave out. When Cyrus decreed that the Jews could return to their holy city of Jerusalem, Daniel had a part in that. When Nehemiah went back to lead the rebuilding of the broken walls of Jerusalem, Daniel had a part in that. When Ezra went back and reestablished respect for the Word of God, Daniel had a part in that. And five hundred years later, when the wise men followed the star making their way to Bethlehem from the East, if you examine it closely, Daniel's witness to their forefathers had a part in that. Those Magi knew about a coming Messiah because their ancestors had heard through the uncompromising life of a young Hebrew captive by the name of Daniel.

Yes, "Daniel continued." And God gave him favor and enlarged his sphere of influence. The apostle Paul noted that each of us has been assigned a specific sphere of influence. He said we should "boast only with regard to the area of influence God [has] assigned to us," and he prayed that "our area of influence among you may be greatly enlarged" (2 Corinthians 10:13, 15 ESV). Etymologically, our English word *influence* comes from a compound of two Latin words that are translated *in* and *flow*. The word picture describes a crystal clear and mighty river that runs deep and wide. Its rapid current powerfully flows and circumvents any and all obstacles in its way. It is fed by numerous smaller creeks, streams, and tributaries that arrive at this river, virtually empty themselves into it, and are caught up in its flow. Having influence means that you live your life in such a deep and vibrant manner that those who come into contact with you become caught up in your flow that reflects and leads them to God's flow. This should serve as a tremendous encouragement to any and all of us seeking to address a twenty-first-century Babylonian culture in our own Western world. Yes, "Daniel continued," and an entire culture eventually got caught up in his flow. May we follow in Daniel's footsteps and impact our culture for the Lord.

A FATHER AT OUR SIDE

One of the joys of my life was being called "pastor" by the wonderful fellowship of believers known as the First Baptist Church in Dallas. For years and years, those generous and foresighted people invested in their young people by sending our youth choirs on mission trips literally around the world. In 1992, they were featured at the Summer Olympic Games in Barcelona, Spain. Those who remember those Olympic Games have forever etched in their memories the 400-meter run.

The favorite to win the gold medal was a strapping young man named Derek Redmond. In the middle of his race, though, Derek suddenly fell. When he finally fought his way back to his feet, he immediately grabbed the back of his leg. He was clearly in great pain. In a split second, a torn hamstring brought a miserable end to years of training and a lifetime of dreams. But Derek Redmond didn't give in, give up, or give out. He got up. He began to hop around the track on one leg. When he reached the final stretch, a large man broke through the security guards and ran right onto the track. He was wearing a T-shirt that asked, "Have you hugged your kid today?" The man put his arm around Derek's waist, Derek put his arm on the man's shoulders, and together they stumbled toward the finish line. The man, it turned out, was Derek Redmond's father, Jim Redmond. It made for a beautiful and memorable picture and a YouTube video that has been viewed by millions. There on the track was a fallen hero with a loving father who made sure his son finished his race. And anyone who witnessed that scene on television that day never forgot it.

Derek Redmond is really a picture of many of us. Some of us are lying on the track of life with our dreams smashed and our hopes dashed. But if we look closely enough, from out of the stands comes a loving Father who takes our arm, puts it over His own shoulders, and helps us along the way. He will see us to the finish line if we simply surrender to Him. Like Derek Redmond we, too, have hope if we don't give out and stay persistent.

Don't Grab the Remote from His Hand

If Daniel 1 tells us anything, it is that God is not removed from the events of human history. He is not sitting in a rocking chair somewhere with His hands folded, twiddling His thumbs. He is here. Right now. Awake and aware and at work. And He has the remote control in His hand. I have, for instance, known brilliant individuals, filled with promise, who gave in to the culture in compromising ways and watched as God lowered the volume of their influence so they could no longer be heard. Others for whom God pushed the Pause button in life have experienced His turning the volume back up, giving them a second chance. This great God was not only active behind the scenes in Daniel's world; He is active in ours as well.

Like Daniel's world, ours is a world that is out of control. We are living in a culture that no longer shares our belief system and is virtually opposed to almost all we believe and hold dear. And this culture is busy at work, right now, reeducating our own most promising and brightest young people. But there is hope: Daniel lived to see the fall of the pagan empire of his day. And Daniel's God is our God. He never changes.

What does Daniel's experience mean to those of us living in a Babylon today? First, because God was in ultimate control did not mean that Daniel remained passive and did nothing. Daniel worked, he prayed, he studied, he took a stand . . . and in the process he influenced a king. Daniel made his choice. He "purposed in his heart." And he "continued" (Daniel 1:9, 21). He never gave in. He never gave up. He never gave out. Daniel wants you to know that you can make it too.

So tomorrow, when you are tempted to give in to the culture, be resistant. Purpose in your own heart today which way you will turn at at life's intersections. And remember that it is never wrong to do right. When you feel so overwhelmed by cultural pressures and are tempted to give up, be consistent. Let your life keep matching what your lips speak. And when you are tempted to just quit, don't give out; be persistent. Cling to the words of Daniel 1:21: "Thus Daniel continued." Insert your own name in place of Daniel's.

As you are reading these words, are you holding tight to the remote control of your own life, seeking to control everything around you as well as your volume, your brightness, everything? Let it go. Hand the remote control of life over to good and gracious God and say, "Lord, here it is. You take control of my life." And then, like Daniel, "purpose in your heart" to continue walking with God whatever the culture says or demands. Daniel's God is your God. And your God—your heavenly Father—is at your side. Don't give out on your walk of faith: be persistent.

SECTION II

Instant Replay

Back to the Future

*O*ne of my favorite people is Dick Lowe. To say that he is a football fan is a gross understatement. He is a bona fide football fanatic . . . especially when it comes to our favorite team, TCU. Dick played for Texas Christian University during his college years, and over these past decades, he has earned the right to be known as "Mr. TCU Football." He led the way in the building of the beautiful new stadium in Fort Worth, and he will be forever remembered due to the bronze statue of him and his wife, Mary, that stands today at the main entrance to the stadium.

During these recent years of TCU's national acclaim and its ranking in the top five football programs in the nation, Dick has been the most visible and vocal fan. Not long ago, we played a longtime rival. It was a high-scoring game that TCU eventually won by a score of 55–52 on the final play of the game. Dick records all the games, and when I asked him a few days after the event, he told me he had viewed that final play at least a half dozen times.

As I sat down to write this chapter of *The Daniel Code*,

which relates to Daniel 2, I thought about Dick Lowe watching that final play so many times after his team's victory. And then I thought how interesting it would have been if we had watched the recording of the game before it was actually played. Think about it. Just imagine that you had watched that video several times before the kick-off and already knew how it was all going to end. You already knew what events and what major plays would lead up to the final whistle that ended the game.

Now, suppose you attended the game and sat in the stands next to your friends and fellow fans. The game moves into the fourth and final quarter, and it is not looking good for your team. But it's clear to your friends that you are not one bit concerned. Why not? Because you have already watched the recording; you know what comes next. Your friends and fans all around you are screaming, wringing their hands, stomping their feet, throwing their hats down on the ground, and even yelling at the referee at the top of their lungs. And you? You just sit there with a slight smile on your face.

Now, that video of a game before the game is played is exactly what we find in Daniel 2. God shows us a recording of the biggest game in world history. He allows us to see how our world culture and history play out the final minutes of the game of life. He takes us through the fourth quarter and all the way to the end of the game. He lets us see that, in fact, we do win in the end. And God tells us all this before it actually happens!

The Author of History

Our world changed forever on September 11, 2001. Radical Islam and its terror tactics are now on the march, and news of terrorist attacks around the world are regular occurrences today. Nuclear weapons are in the hands of rogue nations and aggressively sought by numerous terrorist organizations. Many are worried. Others are wringing their hands in fear. Some are stomping their feet and shouting at the top of their lungs. But we who have seen the recording of the game in Daniel 2 can remain calm and heed the words of James in the New Testament: "Be patient . . . until the coming of the Lord" (James 5:7).

Daniel 2 takes us back to the future, so to speak. God lays out for all posterity, in this one chapter of Scripture, the whole game plan for human history, and He reveals how He remains in control and how His people win in the end. This is valuable and vital information for those of us seeking to stand in a culture that is increasingly running contrary to our convictions and principles. Prophets of doom forecast the end of time with talk of blood moons and a myriad of other prophecies. All sorts of scriptures are perverted and perceived as relevant to many events in the news. When we see news from around the world, it seems we are indeed living in the fourth quarter of human history, and time may be running out.

Daniel 2 is one of the most remarkable and amazing chapters in all the Bible. Here is a young man who lived twenty-five hundred years ago, and God not only reveals through him what has taken place in the last two and a half millennia but also what is going on in our world right now. As Daniel told King Nebuchadnezzar, "There is a God in heaven who reveals secrets," and he went on to tell the king accurately "what will be in the latter days" (Daniel 2:28–29 ESV). We are introduced to the image of a statue and a stone that hold the key to the unfolding of world history and its ultimate climax, the return of the Lord Jesus Christ to planet Earth. Reading Daniel's prophecy is like watching that recording of the football game before it is even played. And so there will be no uncertainty about the authority of the message, God spoke through Daniel that the dream "is certain and its interpretation is sure" (v. 45).

The first thirty verses of Daniel 2 are a narrative about King Nebuchadnezzar having a terrible, nightmarish dream. In his dream he saw a great statue and then a great stone. The stone smashed the statue's feet and brought the whole statue crumbling to earth. Then the stone in his dream filled the entire earth.

Being troubled by his dream, Nebuchadnezzar called together all the wise men of his kingdom, including astrologers, magicians, seers, and sorcerers, and demanded they tell him not only what he had dreamed but also an interpretation. Of course the wise men failed miserably. So he did what most wicked kings would do in such a situation: he ordered that all of them be put to death. Daniel and his three Hebrew friends—Shadrach, Meshach, and Abed-Nego—were among this group of wise men. But just in the nick of time "the secret was revealed to Daniel in a night vision" (Daniel 2:19), so Daniel went before the king and laid out the dream and its meaning to him, explaining, "There is a God in heaven who reveals secrets, and He has made known to King Nebuchadnezzar what will be in the latter days" (v. 28).

OUR GOD REIGNS

In our own uncertain times and as we seek to engage a crumbling culture in a twenty-first-century world, this is an important reminder to us: there is still a God in heaven who "reveals secrets." He has not abdicated His throne. Much like Daniel, we live in a culture that is increasingly hostile to what we believe and hold dear—but "there is a God in heaven!" Our children and grandchildren face a world totally unlike the world we grew up in and one we couldn't have imagined—but there is still a God in heaven!

We are about to see not only Daniel's interpretation of the king's dream in the following chapters, but also its stunning application for us today. When we understand this dream, lay it alongside world history books and the morning news, we see that God's Word is as much alive and applicable today as ever.

Remember, Daniel is teaching us how to find our way through a modern culture that is rapidly losing its way. He is about to show us a panorama of world history to assure us that we are on the winning side even in those darkest of days when victory seems so remote. And this reassurance provides us with the confidence to enter the marketplace of culture and stand strong with the assurance that we are the ones who are going to win in the end.

After we view this recording of human history before it actually takes place and when we understand Daniel's interpretation of the king's dream, we will enjoy the game of life with a lot less stress, fear, and tension. We will—like Daniel—be more able to live out our days without giving in, giving up, or giving out.

God reveals two truths in Daniel 2: the *scope* of human history with a statue and the *hope* of human history with a stone. It's time to click the Play button on the remote control and view the big game before the kick-off even takes place.

5 GOD REVEALS THE SCOPE OF HUMAN HISTORY

Part 1

"You, O king, were watching; and behold, a great image! This great image, whose splendor was excellent, stood before you; and its form was awesome. This image's head was of fine gold, its chest and arms of silver, its belly and thighs[a] of bronze, its legs of iron, its feet partly of iron and partly of clay. You watched while a stone was cut out without hands, which struck the image on its feet of iron and clay, and broke them in pieces. Then the iron, the clay, the bronze, the silver, and the gold were crushed together, and became like chaff from the summer threshing floors; the wind carried them away so that no trace of them was found. And the stone that struck the image became a great mountain and filled the whole earth.

"This is the dream. Now we will tell the interpretation of it before the king. You, O king, are a king of kings. For the God of heaven has given you a kingdom, power, strength, and glory; and wherever the children of men dwell, or the beasts of the field and the birds of the heaven, He has given them into your hand, and has made you ruler over them all—you are this head of gold. But after you shall arise another kingdom inferior to yours; then another, a third kingdom of bronze, which shall *rule over all the earth. And the fourth kingdom shall be as strong as iron, inasmuch as iron breaks in pieces and shatters everything; and like iron that crushes, that kingdom will break in pieces and crush all the others. Whereas you saw the feet and toes, partly of potter's clay and partly of iron, the kingdom shall be divided; yet the strength of the iron shall be in it, just as you saw the iron mixed with ceramic clay. And as the toes of the feet were partly of iron and partly of clay, so the kingdom shall be partly strong and partly fragile. As you saw iron mixed with ceramic clay, they will mingle with the seed of men; but they will not adhere to one another, just as iron does not mix with clay."*

—DANIEL 2:31–43

*I*f you could pick one spot in all the world to go and sit for a minute, where would you go?

I don't have to give that question a second thought. I would definitely go right to the summit of the Mount of Olives in Jerusalem. When you sit there, you see one of the most beautiful panoramas on the entire earth. From that very spot, the psalmist wrote that Jerusalem was "beautiful in its loftiness, the joy of the whole earth" (Psalm 48:2 NIV). Looking to the left on a clear day, you can see the mountains of Bethlehem. Then moving your gaze to the right, you come to Mount Zion and the citadel of David's city. Straight ahead and across the Kidron Valley below is Mount Moriah. There at the southeastern corner of the old walled city, you see the pinnacle of the temple and the Temple Mount itself, where once stood the glory of the massive and magnificent Jewish temple. Today on that spot resides the Dome of the Rock, glistening in the Middle Eastern sun. Before you is the Eastern Gate of the walled city, which has been there for centuries. Continuing your gaze toward the north you'll see Mount Scopus, and beyond it on another, more distant mountain is the tomb of Samuel the prophet. It is an amazing and beautiful view.

As we arrive at Daniel 2, we find ourselves standing on a tall mountaintop of Scripture, viewing the panorama of the chapter in world history encompassing what Jesus called "the times of the Gentiles" (Luke 21:24). It covers a time period from 605 BC until the consummation of the age, when the Lord Jesus returns as the King of all kings and the Lord of all lords. God Himself stepped right into the dream of an ancient Babylonian king in order to reveal to us our future—the entire scope of human history—through the image of a statue. And of course we have several questions.

Now, About That Dream . . .

What exactly did Nebuchadnezzar dream, and *what* did Daniel interpret it to mean? Central to the king's dream was a statue made of gold, silver, bronze, iron, and clay. Twice it is called "great," and it must have been an awesome sight. It was the image of a man whose head was gold, chest and arms were silver, abdomen was bronze, legs were iron, and its feet and toes were a mixture of iron and clay. The statue had a limited lifetime: its ultimate destiny was the utter destruction that came suddenly and surely when a great stone demolished it and then filled the whole earth.

So *who* does this image represent? Daniel got specific in verses 36–43, but anyone who knows world history from 600 BC until the present day knows that there have been four dominant world empires. In 605 BC, the Babylonian Empire was reaching its zenith. In 539 BC, the great Medo-Persian Empire diverted the Euphrates River and entered the great walled city of Babylon by night. After only sixty-five years of world dominance, Babylon fell virtually overnight. Next, in 331 BC, a young Greek named Alexander swept across the world of his day, and the Greek Empire ruled the known world. But in 146 BC, the Roman legions began their conquest, crushing everything and everyone in their path. All these world empires were represented in the king's dream— centuries before they were ever heard of.

First, Daniel interpreted the "head of gold" as Babylon herself. Babylon was well known for its gold. The ancient historian Herodotus visited Babylon and wrote that he had never seen such a proliferation of gold. He saw golden temples, golden altars, golden gates, and even golden walkways. Nebuchadnezzar had built a golden city complete with his own golden throne. So that there would be no doubt as to the image's meaning, Daniel stood before the king and exclaimed, "You are this head of gold" (Daniel 2:38).

Who, then, is the chest and arms of silver? Unquestionably, it is the Medo-Persian Empire. Daniel revealed to the king that coming after him a new kingdom would arise (Daniel 2:39). And so it was: the Medes and Persians defeated the Babylonian Empire and became the next world power under Cyrus. From the book of Esther, we learn that these Persian rulers would dominate the world. The two arms represent the Medes and the Persians in this coalition, and world history records these events just as Daniel had foreseen them.

MOVING ALONG

Next in the body of this image we come to the abdomen of bronze, representing the Greek Empire. How do we know this? Just as foretold, the Greeks defeated the Medes and the Persians in 334 BC after Alexander took the throne of Greece at only twenty years of age. He died at thirty-two, weeping over the fact that "there were no more worlds to conquer." God identified this very kingdom even by name in Daniel 8:21 and 11:2. The Greeks were well known for their use of bronze and brass: their helmets, breastplates, and shields were made of such metals. The Greeks' contributions to world culture are beyond description. Herodotus stands without peer as the father of historians. Hippocrates is the father of modern medicine. Socrates, Plato, and Aristotle have helped shape philosophy for centuries. The amazing thing is how God spoke of all these world powers long before they existed. We are watching through Daniel the recording before the game is even played.

Then came the "legs of iron." There is zero doubt about the identity of this empire. Here we see the great Roman

Empire rise to dominate the world for the next few centuries and rule with an iron hand. Rome was ruthless; it broke in pieces and shattered every nation in its path (Daniel 2:40). Iron was the symbol of strength, and this empire more than lived up to its name. Rome is expressed in the two legs of iron because this great power would divide into two, Rome in the west and Constantinople, modern-day Istanbul, in the east, where it became known as the great Byzantine Empire. The monarchies of France, Germany, Spain, and later Great Britain were the result of the western spread of the Roman Empire. Our own Western world here in America is Roman in its roots. It is imprinted in our own history. Our senate, our representative form of government, our courts, our laws, and our military all reflect the influence of the ancient Roman Empire. And it is worth nothing that Rome was never defeated; she collapsed from a corrupt culture within. But she still lives on in the ideals adopted and preserved by the Western world.

Finally, this image had feet and toes that were a mixture of iron and clay. These toes represent the continuation of Rome. The Bible reveals that a coalition—a federation of nations—would arise out of the ruins of the Roman Empire. These nations would mix the iron and clay; that is, the ideas of totalitarianism/imperialism and the principles of democracy that are more pliable and can be molded like clay. Great Britain and the United States are illustrative of this fact.

Two important questions about Nebuchadnezzar's dream and its meaning remain—*when* and *why*—which we will unpack in the next chapter. Before turning the page, think on this truth: the greatest proof we have that the Bible is true is the way prophecy is foretold and then fulfilled, both consistently and in startling detail, throughout its pages. The Bible is indeed a miraculous and amazing book.

God Reveals the Scope of Human History

Part 2

*T*he statue of the image of a man in Nebuchadnezzar's dream reveals to us the entire scope of history for the past twenty-six hundred years. Rome is the last real world empire, but the modern Western world—represented in the feet and toes of this awesome image—is a continuation of Rome in many ways. The past has seen the likes of Napoleon, Stalin, Hitler, and the more modern Islamic Caliphate set their sights on world domination. And they left millions dead in their attempts to do so. But, in the end, they all failed.

Past, Present, Future

The question arises as to why the last two thousand years seem to be omitted from the message of this image. This matter brings us to our third question: *When* is the timeline here in play? The image and interpretation seem to pass over the time between Roman dominion when Christ first came to earth and the time when the stone strikes the statue in its feet, representing the second coming of Christ and the eventual end of the age. Bible scholars do not find it surprising that there is silence here. The Old Testament never foresaw the church age: it was hidden. Paul himself wrote in Greek that it was a *musterion*, that is, a sacred secret, a mystery. But in the last days, a confederation of nations will arise out of the old Roman Empire. Daniel said that these nations were the ten toes of Nebuchadnezzar's image. The apostle John, the Revelator, referred to them as the ten kings in Revelation 17. Before Christ returns, a coalition of nations, arising out of the old Roman Empire, will emerge with talk of a one-world government. Out of them will arise an electrifying world leader who will promise to free the entire world of economic problems and bring about a lasting peace. In Scripture he is called the Antichrist.

Some people have been quick to point to the European Common Market as the coalition mentioned in Daniel's prophecies. After all, we saw a divided Europe unite virtually overnight with the collapse of the Berlin Wall and the end of the Cold War. Today, Europe has a common currency, and Israel is back in her own land, controlling the city of Jerusalem for the first time since the days of Nebuchadnezzar. The stage is being set and the props are being put into place for the climactic event of human history: the visible return of Jesus Christ to planet Earth, an event revealed over two and a half millennia ago.

Now, it is interesting and significant to note that this statue's structure weakens as it moves from head to toe. Look at it carefully. The statue is obviously top-heavy and then weak in its feet. We see here the downward spiral of human existence. Note also the deteriorating elements, from gold to silver to bronze to iron to mud and finally to clay. This, too, strongly suggests the degeneration of the human race through the ages. This appears diametrically opposed to evolutionist thought and its interpretation of human history. We are not getting better. Oh, we may have more sophisticated conveniences than the ancients did, but we are getting worse morally, not better. Darwinian thought suggests we are ascending and improving, but God says—and history actually shows—just the opposite.

The "when" of Daniel's prophecy is laid out plain and clear: God has a plan. History is unfolding on His time schedule. And He revealed the scope of that history with a statue thousands of years ago.

A WORD OF WARNING

We now arrive at the crucial question, *why* this statue? What the king dreamed and what Daniel revealed was—in the words of Jesus—"the times of the Gentiles" (Luke 21:24). The time period between the Babylonian conquest of Jerusalem and the second coming of Christ is when, for much of the time, Israel was a people scattered throughout the world.

God had commended the government of the world to Israel. It was to be administered by priests, godly prophets, and good kings, but Israel repeatedly disobeyed. Thus God called an intermission and handed over the governments of the world to the Gentiles. This "times of the Gentiles" corresponded to the days of human history when Israel was without a king. The ancient prophet Hosea framed it thus:

"For the children of Israel shall abide many days without king or prince, without sacrifice or sacred pillar. . . . Afterward the children of Israel shall return and seek the LORD their God and . . . they shall fear the LORD and His goodness in the latter days" (Hosea 3:4–5). And those "latter days" seem fast approaching. King Jesus will return. He will end the times of the Gentiles, establish afresh and anew His kingdom in Israel, and reign and rule for a millennium of perfect peace.

Yes, the stage is set today. Many of the major players have been put in place in our lifetime. Israel is back in her land—and that is no small accomplishment after centuries of exile and dispersion. This player was put in place in 1948, and her role became more significant in 1967, when she took control of Jerusalem. For the first time since Nebuchadnezzar entered and destroyed the city, Israel began ruling her own land. At this writing, dramatic events are unfolding in the Middle East as well as in Europe. The coalition of "iron and clay" is coming together.

Yet even though Israel is back in her promised land, there stands in her holy city a stark reminder that she still is living in "the times of the Gentiles." Ask any Jew if they still feel Gentile oppression. Even though they are now a generation removed from the Holocaust, they still experience persecution, and harsh public opinion is constantly fueled by a coalition of Gentile nations commonly referred to as the United Nations. Furthermore, walk through the Dung Gate of the old walled city of Jerusalem and step upon the Temple

Mount. What do you see? The Mosque of Omar, more commonly called the Dome of the Rock and the third holiest site in the Muslim world. The Jews may have successfully and miraculously won a string of modern wars and conflicts, but they have never gotten to their holiest spot, the Temple Mount. That mosque stands to remind the Jews daily that they are still living in the "times of the Gentiles."

GOD IS IN CONTROL

God is allowing mankind to fully experience the consequences of our choices. It appears we are hell-bent on destroying both our world and civilization as we have known it. This seems to be true morally, economically, biologically, meteorologically, environmentally, and virtually every other way imaginable. And just when it looks like hope is almost gone—this is God's message to us through Nebuchadnezzar's dream and Daniel's interpretation of it— the stone will come out of heaven, smash the statue, and then fill the entire earth. Jesus Christ, the Rock of Ages, will return, demolish all world powers, and fill the earth with His own glorious kingdom.

What does all this prophecy have to do with us as we seek to engage our culture for good? It should have the same effect on you and me that it had on Daniel. The image of that statue reminds us that God is still in control; that we can trust Him; and that everything in human history has unfolded exactly as Nebuchadnezzar dreamed and Daniel revealed. And what is yet to be fulfilled will follow suit. We have seen in Daniel 2 the recording before the game is even played and God is in control. With a statue He revealed the scope of human history to us . . . and the fact that we win in the end.

Yes, we—like Daniel—can find our way in a culture that has lost its way.

7 GOD REVEALS THE HOPE OF HUMAN HISTORY

Part 1

"You watched while a stone was cut out without hands, which struck the image on its feet of iron and clay, and broke them in pieces. Then the iron, the clay, the bronze, the silver, and the gold were crushed together, and became like chaff from the summer threshing floors; the wind carried them away so that no trace of them was found. And the stone that struck the image became a great mountain and filled the whole earth. . . .

"And in the days of these kings the God of heaven will set up a kingdom which shall never be destroyed; and the kingdom shall not be left to other people; it shall break in pieces and consume all these kingdoms, and it shall stand forever. Inasmuch as you saw that the stone was cut out of the mountain without hands, and that it broke in pieces the iron, the bronze, the clay, the silver, and the gold—the great God has made known to the king what will come to pass after this. The dream is certain, and its interpretation is sure."

—DANIEL 2:34–35, 44–45

*I*n Daniel's own words, "The dream is certain, and its interpretation is sure" (Daniel 2:45). When this confederation of nations arising primarily out of the old Roman Empire emerges on the world scene, this stone—"cut out . . . without hands" (v. 45)—from Daniel's interpretation of the king's dream comes out of heaven and strikes the statue at its feet, bringing it to the ground. The statue crumbles, indicating the virtual end of the world as we know it. Then the stone grows into a great mountain and fills the earth, representing the coming kingdom of our Lord that will be universal and will stand forever! As with the statue, this stone raises some critical questions.

WHO?

First, *who* is represented by this stone? On this point the Scriptures speak clearly. The psalmist wrote, "The stone which the builders rejected has become the chief cornerstone" (Psalm 118:22). The prophet Isaiah said, "He will be as a sanctuary, but a stone of stumbling and a rock of offense to both the houses of Israel" (Isaiah 8:14). To Israel, the Lord Jesus Christ was a "stone of stumbling." Israel was looking for a political messiah to free them from Roman rule and oppression, but Jesus came the first time as a suffering Servant and riding on a donkey, not a white stallion. The cornerstone of God's plan for salvation, Jesus was outright rejected by the Jewish builders. Matthew recorded Jesus' repetition of the words of the psalmist: "The stone which the builders rejected has become the chief cornerstone" (Matthew 21:42). Then Jesus Himself prophesied, "On whomever this stone falls it will grind him to powder" (v. 44). Who is this stone in Daniel 2:34? It is none other than Jesus Christ Himself.

Then Daniel got specific: this stone was "cut out without hands" (Daniel 2:34). That is, it was supernatural in its origin. Neither human hands nor human means brought it into existence. We New Testament believers know that Jesus was there before "the beginning" (John 1:1–2, 14) and that when He came to earth, He clothed Himself in human flesh. No human made that happen: Jesus was miraculously born of a virgin. This stone in the king's dream is the Lord Jesus—and He is the only hope of all of human history.

WHAT?

What unusual event is represented by the stone striking the statue? It is the second coming of our Lord. When He returns, it will be with great power and glory. Handel's classic masterpiece the "Hallelujah" chorus captures the sense of joy and glory John described in Revelation, written while he was exiled on Patmos: "The kingdoms of this world have become the kingdoms of our Lord and of His Christ, and He shall reign forever and ever" (11:15). The greatest fact of Bible prophecy is that Jesus is coming back visibly, bodily, and personally to this earth. Palm Sunday was not the last journey Jesus will ever make down the Mount of Olives, across the Kidron Valley, and through the Eastern Gate of the city. He is coming back . . . and won't be riding a donkey this time, but, as a conquering King, will be mounted on a white stallion. Yes, "He [will] strike the nations. And He Himself will rule them" (19:15).

The entire Bible testifies of Jesus' glorious return. The angels at the Ascension foretold it, saying, "Men of Galilee, why do you stand gazing up into heaven? This same Jesus, who was taken up from you into heaven, will so come in like manner as you saw Him go into heaven" (Acts 1:11). Jesus' return is spoken of when Paul's words are quoted before Communion: "For as often as you eat this bread and drink this cup, you proclaim the Lord's death till He comes" (1 Corinthians 11:26). And the night before the crucifixion, Jesus foretold it: "In My Father's house are many mansions; if it were not so, I would have told you. I go to prepare a place for you. And if I go and prepare a place for you, I will come again and receive you to Myself; that where I am, there you may be also" (John 14:2–3). The knowledge of this future event fills us believers with hope as we seek to engage a corrupt and corroding culture while we wait.

WHERE?

As we return to Nebuchadnezzar's dream, it is important to note *where* the stone struck the statue. It did not strike the head: our Lord did not return to rule and reign during the Babylonian supremacy. Nor did the stone strike the chest or the abdomen, where most of our vital organs are encased. Jesus did not come during the time of the Medes, the Persians, or the Greeks. And the stone did not strike the legs.

Now, anyone who has ever played football knows that the first rule for tackling an opposing player is to knock his legs out from under him. But, again, our Lord did not set up His kingdom during the world dominance of Rome. The stone clearly strikes the feet, the last stage of Gentile world domination, and these are the very days in which we are living right now. When our Lord returns, human history as we know it will come to an end. Nothing will remain of the statue but dust that will be blown away by the wind.

WHEN?

So *when* will all this take place? When will the stone strike the feet of the statue? When will Jesus return and establish His reign and the preeminence of His people? This end of "the times of the Gentiles" will happen when the remnant of the last great world power emerges in a multinational confederacy.

Time and again it has appeared that the fulfillment of this prophecy might be unfolding. It once looked as though Napoleon Bonaparte would conquer the world and make France a great world empire. But he met his Waterloo, so to speak, and later died alone as a refugee on the rocky isle of Helena. Why? Because God had determined that Rome would be the last world empire. Hitler made some astonishing claims about world dominion, but before he accomplished it, he died in his bunker by his own hand while Berlin went up in flames. When I was a boy, I heard Nikita Khrushchev say that America would crumble in the Soviet Union's own hands, and I lived to see the day his own empire imploded overnight.

As we read Daniel and confront our own crumbling culture, we are reminded of the futility of putting our faith in human governments. They are all destined to go the way of those before them: onto the ash heap of time. Our only hope is in a stone "not cut with human hands." The Lord Jesus will one day return, and when He does, He will fill the earth with His peace and His glory. No wonder the last line of the Bible is the plea, "Even so, come, Lord Jesus" (Revelation 22:20).

8   GOD REVEALS THE HOPE
   OF HUMAN HISTORY

Part 2

*A*s Daniel 2 comes to an end, we discover that—unlike the title of the movie—the empire does *not* strike back. It strikes out instead! If human history has taught us anything, it is that all world empires are temporary. One comes after another. None ever strike back; they all strike out.

How

Having just dealt with the who, what, where, and when of this stone in Nebuchadnezzar's dream, we now arrive at the "how" question: How will this great statue fall? We see the stone strike it with destructive force. The statue shatters; it breaks apart. The stone crushes the statue. This crushing of a world power is not going to be led by the meek and mild Jesus nonchalantly riding toward Jerusalem on the back of a swayback donkey. This is King Jesus coming to rule and reign . . . forever! In His apocalyptic discourse on the Mount of Olives, Jesus said, "Then the sign of the Son of Man will appear in heaven, and all the tribes of the earth will mourn, and they will see the Son of Man coming on the clouds of the heaven, with power and great glory" (Matthew 24:30). The kingdoms of this world will be crushed. Utter destruction will be the lot of all the world systems. The judgment of God is coming—and as Daniel reminds us, "The dream is certain, and its interpretation is sure" (Daniel 2:45).

WHY?

Finally, we come to the "why" question, knowing that God always has a purpose in what He does. He is never taken by surprise, and nothing happens by accident. So why was the statue—why are all the nations—destroyed? God was destroying—and He will destroy—the old. Why? To bring in the new.

Exiled on Patmos, the apostle John said, "Now I saw a new heaven and a new earth, for the first heaven and the first earth had passed away. Also there was no more sea. Then I, John, saw the holy city, New Jerusalem, coming down out of heaven from God, prepared as a bride adorned for her husband" (Revelation 21:1–2). God is going to cleanse this planet, set up His earthly kingdom, and then usher in eternity: the stone will grow and fill the whole world. Our Lord is going to return to our war-weary, terrorist-tormented world during the "ten toes" of Daniel's prophecy. When He does, He will help us right our world and end "the times of the Gentiles."

Daniel revealed that the stone that strikes the statue in Nebuchadnezzar's dream becomes a "great mountain" (Daniel 2:35). This picture foretells that the kingdom of God will one day fill the entire earth. Knowledgeable commentators see this as the great millennial reign of Christ. In that day, men will "beat their swords into plowshares and their spears into pruning hooks" (Isaiah 2:4). John spoke to this point, reminding us that "the kingdoms of this world have become the kingdoms of our Lord and of His Christ, and He shall reign forever and ever" (Revelation 11:15). The psalmist saw this day a thousand years earlier and said, "All kings shall fall down before Him; all nations shall serve Him" (Psalm 72:11). In New Testament times, Paul spoke of it when writing to the Philippians: "At the name of Jesus every knee should bow, of those in heaven, and of those on earth, and of those under the earth, and that every tongue should confess that Jesus Christ is Lord, to the glory of God the Father" (Philippians 2:10–11). When we pray the model prayer Jesus gave us, this coming kingdom is the very subject of our petition: "Your kingdom come, Your will be done on earth as it is in heaven" (Luke 11:2).

Right now the Gentile rule of earth is disintegrating and degenerating with every passing generation. We human beings are not getting better. Like the statue, we are getting weaker and wobblier as time goes on. Yet the Jews are back in their land. So many other prophesied players are being set in place even as you read these words. The end is fast approaching. This stone—the Lord Jesus—will return to set up His eternal kingdom.

The Scope and the Hope of History

Daniel 2 ends with Daniel becoming the virtual prime minister of Babylon because of his interpretation of this dream (Daniel 2:46–49). And Nebuchadnezzar made this startling confession: "Truly your God is the God of gods, the Lord of kings, and a revealer of secrets" (v. 47). Sadly, he couldn't say, "Your God is my God" but only your God is "a god." Human beings haven't changed much across these centuries. Most of our world, if they acknowledge the Lord at all, see Him merely as some nebulous, unknown force existing within everything or everyone.

This encounter between Daniel and the Babylonian culture should serve as an energizing encouragement to us as we seek to live in the midst of our own pagan culture. God has revealed to us the *scope* of human history in a statue. We don't have to wonder about the outcome; we can be sure we are on the winning team. And God revealed to us the *hope* of human history in a stone. The kingdoms of this world rise up and bark for a while, but they are only temporary. Babylon, the great city of gold, fell and never rose again. We know it as Iraq today. The Babylonian Empire died. Our Lord died also—but He rose again and is coming back to rule and reign. In fact, it was this second coming and not the first that hymn writer Isaac Watts actually had in mind when he wrote what we sing during the Christmas season each year: "Joy to the world! The Lord is come. Let earth receive her King." And he concluded the song saying, "He rules the world with truth and grace, and makes the nations prove the glories of His righteousness and wonders of His love!"

BACK TO THE FUTURE

Yes, my buddy Dick Lowe watched that recording of the football game several times even though it had already happened. In sharp contrast we have here in Daniel an account of the ultimate event in human history—Jesus' return—and we can watch this recording again and again even though it hasn't happened yet. Knowing the ending of history takes the fear and suspense out of life. While others wring their hands, stomp their feet, and desperately want to know what to do, we have already seen how it all is going to end. We can therefore find our way through a culture that is losing its way with each passing day. Yes, "there is a God in heaven who reveals secrets" (Daniel 2:28). And this great God has not abdicated His throne. He is in charge of all of human history . . . and that involves your history and mine as well.

SECTION III
YOU HAVE WHAT YOU TOLERATE

*T*hroughout my life I have made it a practice to count among my close friends several men who were some years my senior. I have gleaned much from their experience and wisdom. Most of them have moved on to their eternal reward as the years have passed by. One of these men whom I didn't get to know until his dying days was Jack Evans. This successful CEO of a major corporation and former mayor of the city of Dallas lifted me up each time I was with him. Jack coined a saying that still hangs on wall plaques in the offices of many business leaders in our city as well as my own. His often repeated saying is, "You have what you tolerate."

I thought about Jack Evans when I sat down to write about this old and familiar story of the three Hebrew young men who stood true to their personal convictions yet ended up in a burning fiery furnace because they refused to tolerate their culture's pressure to worship a false god. We'll get to those three in a bit.

"You have what you tolerate" is true in every area of life. Parents who tolerate their kids talking back to them and disobeying eventually reap young adults who have little respect for authority. It is true in the classroom: teachers who tolerate sloppy work and missing assignments end up with students who cannot pass the final exam. It is all too obvious in sports as well: coaches who tolerate undisciplined practices see the results when game day rolls around. And in business, those companies that tolerate mediocrity and are content to be reactive instead of proactive will lose productivity in the long run. Yes, Jack Evans had it right: you have what you tolerate!

Our culture has tolerated things for so long that Jack Evans's words have proved all too true: we are simply experiencing today the consequences of what we tolerated yesterday. *Tolerance* is the new buzzword and the new law of the land, and it has a different definition than it did just a few years ago. *Tolerance* used to mean that we recognized and respected other people's beliefs and value systems without agreeing with them or sharing them. Today *tolerance* means that everyone's values, belief systems, and lifestyles should be accepted. Tolerance shouts that all truth claims are valid and equal. In fact, in our current culture, the worst thing that can be said of someone is that he or she is intolerant. Our culture continues to slowly and surely try to form all of us into its mold of being completely tolerant of everything—and we will end up having what we tolerate.

Our Intolerant Lord

Cable news outlets are a phenomenon of our contemporary culture. A myriad of television talk shows are available twenty-four hours a day on multiple channels. While watching an aggressive debate taking place on one such show recently, I thought, *What if the Lord Jesus were interviewed by one of these talk-show hosts?* If Jesus were to say on a cable talk show today what He said in the Gospels, He would be attacked, ridiculed, and called an intolerant bigot right to His face.

For example, if Jesus were asked about the current breakdown in the American home, what do you think would happen if He gave an answer like He gave to the woman at the well? Speaking to her about her lifestyle, Jesus said, "Go, call your husband, and come here." When she replied she didn't have a husband, He shot back, "You have well said, 'I have no husband,' for you have had five husbands, and the one whom you now have is not your husband" (John 4:15–18). The immediate reply of the talk-show host would be, "Who do You think You are? You are completely intolerant!" And what if, in a conversation concerning the many world religions, Jesus were to say what He said in John 14:6: "I am the way, the truth, and the life. No one comes to the Father except through Me." That is the exact opposite of tolerance, the theme of our day. Our modern culture is screaming at us that everyone's truth claims, values, lifestyles, and the like should be considered equal.

In fact, our culture has no moral absolutes; tolerance has become the only real absolute. One of the favorite scriptures often quoted by proponents of this ideology are the words of Jesus to the woman taken in adultery: "Neither do I condemn you" (John 8:11). Rather conveniently, they always leave out the last part of the verse. Few people seem to want to acknowledge that in the same breath Jesus added, "Go and sin no more"—and this was not merely a suggestion. Its imperative mood and present tense indicate that our Lord forcefully said, "*Stop* your sinning right now! Stop it!" He met this woman where she was—stuck in a sinful lifestyle—but after meeting Him, she didn't stay there. Her life was changed because Jesus would not tolerate or let her tolerate a life of sin.

Like our Lord, we are not to tolerate sin in our lives or sin as a culturally acceptable trait. Yet we are living in a culture that is increasingly hostile to Christianity. Moral values and religious liberties held sacred since our nation's founding are being trampled on. We have today what we tolerated yesterday. And some things should simply not be tolerated. How tolerant do you believe your Muslim neighbors would be in a culture that spoke of Mohammed as the American culture speaks of Jesus today? Recently, a government-sponsored art show in New York City featured as a piece of art a crucifix in a bottle of urine. Not only do we have today what we tolerated yesterday, but we will have tomorrow what we are tolerating today. Why? Jack Evans said it best: you have what you tolerate! And that is a chilling thought.

Standing Up to Intolerance

From time to time throughout history, however, there have been those people who stood up for their beliefs rather than tolerate their culture's intolerance and hostility. Consider the thrilling narrative of the deliverance of the three Hebrew young men from the burning fiery furnace in Babylon. If you are reading these words and find yourself in a tight spot with seemingly no way out, then Daniel 3 is just for you. Shadrach, Meshach, and Abed-Nego's victory is a comfort and a challenge to us in a culture intolerant of our Christian faith. It is the story of faith triumphing over fear. It is the story of courage triumphing over cowardice. It is the story of conviction triumphing over compromise. It is the story of three brave young men who stood faithful to their God despite pressure from their culture.

These young men live on in memory today to teach us some valuable life lessons. God, for instance, never promises us that when we take a stand for Him, we will avoid the fiery-furnace experiences of life. He didn't keep these three faithful followers from that experience. But, as we will soon see, He got in with them and loosed their bonds . . . and He will do the same for you.

In a world screaming at the top of its lungs for tolerance, we will be tested. The decisions we will make this week will be governed by one of two things: inner principle or outer pressure. That is, either by the Word of God or by the world's way of thinking. If we allow God's Word to shape our inner principles, we will respond to life's fiery furnaces with faith that God will ultimately deliver us. But if we allow the world's way of thinking to pressure our decision making, we will react in fear resulting in ultimate defeat. Shadrach, Meshach, and Abed-Nego lived by an inner principle of personal convictions shaped by their God. The people around them were governed only by external pressure to conform, and ultimately . . . they got what they tolerated.

As we seek to find our way through a culture that is losing its way, Daniel has called us to never give in, never give up, and never give out. Now his three Hebrew friends have something to say to us. Let's read on, look at their example, and listen to their wise counsel. After all, Jack Evans's words have never rung more true than in our present day: you have what you tolerate!

9

LIVING WITH PRESSURE

Nebuchadnezzar the king made an image of gold, whose height was sixty cubits and its width six cubits. He set it up in the plain of Dura, in the province of Babylon. And King Nebuchadnezzar sent word to gather together the satraps, the administrators, the governors, the counselors, the treasurers, the judges, the magistrates, and all the officials of the provinces, to come to the dedication of the image which King Nebuchadnezzar had set up. So the satraps, the administrators, the governors, the counselors, the treasurers, the judges, the magistrates, and all the officials of the provinces gathered together for the dedication of the image that King Nebuchadnezzar had set up; and they stood before the image that Nebuchadnezzar had set up. Then a herald cried aloud: "To you it is commanded, O peoples, nations, and languages, that at the time you hear the sound of the horn, flute, harp, lyre, and psaltery, in symphony with all kinds of music, you shall fall down and worship the gold image that King Nebuchadnezzar has set up; and whoever does not fall down and worship shall be cast immediately into the midst of a burning fiery furnace."

So at that time, when all the people heard the sound of the horn, flute, harp, and lyre, in symphony with all kinds of music, all the people, nations, and languages fell down and worshiped the gold image which King Nebuchadnezzar had set up.

Therefore at that time certain Chaldeans came forward and accused the Jews. They spoke and said to King Nebuchadnezzar, "O king, live forever! You, O king, have made a decree that everyone who hears the sound of the horn, flute, harp, lyre, and psaltery, in symphony with all kinds of music, shall fall down and worship the gold image; and whoever does not fall down and worship shall be cast into the midst of a burning fiery furnace. There are certain Jews whom you have set over the affairs of the province of Babylon: Shadrach, Meshach, and Abed-Nego; these men, O king, have not paid due regard to you. They do not serve your gods or worship the gold image which you have set up."

—DANIEL 3:1–12

*O*ne thing is certain: our faith will be tested in our contemptible, contemporary culture just as the Babylonian culture tested Daniel and his friends.

King Nebuchadnezzar erected a huge image out on the plain of Dura in Babylon. It was made of gold and stood nine stories tall. Placed out on the plain, it could be seen for miles as it glistened in the morning sun. It must have been an awesome sight. This magnificent act of self-aggrandizement called for an elaborate dedication ceremony, and it was planned with explicit detail. On the big day, thousands gathered with instructions that when the orchestra began to play, they were to all bow down low to the ground and worship the golden image. Anyone refusing to do so would meet a horrible fate: they would be thrown into a fiery furnace to meet an agonizing end.

It was in this context that Shadrach, Meshach, and Abed-Nego would meet their life's greatest test. Should they go along with the rest of the crowd just this one time? After all, they would be lost in the midst of that vast horde of people. No one would even notice if they bowed. Or should they remain true to their convictions, stand alone, and refuse to bow to any image? That's what their Torah commandments had long taught them. This test has a way of finding all of us sooner or later along our own journey.

There is, after all, a very real sense in which we all live out there on the plain of Dura every week. Our world is calling for tolerance at every turn. We watch as almost everyone else seems to go along with the crowd and bow before the false images. As Daniel recorded this encounter, he called on us who live in a culture gone awry to learn to live with that outer pressure. It is not going away.

BOW—OR BURN!

Woven throughout the paragraphs of Daniel 3 is the theme of peer pressure. All the surrounding nations lived in subjection to mighty Babylon, so they all sent delegations to the dedication festivities. The city was decorated to perfection. It was the single biggest day in all its illustrious history. There, standing over ninety feet tall, was the golden image surrounded—as far as one could see—by a mass of humanity. The signal was given, and the orchestra began to play right on cue. In one fell swoop, everyone got down on their knees and bowed lowed to the golden image. The choice was simple: they could bow or they could burn.

In that crowd all the big shots were assembled alongside the mass of commoners. Daniel referred to "the satraps, the administrators, the governors, the counselors, the treasurers, the judges, the magistrates, and all the officials of the provinces" (Daniel 3:2). Surrendering to the peer pressure, they bowed. I am sure more than one of them was thinking, *I have to keep my job! I need the insurance!* Things haven't changed much across all these centuries. Every week in every city of America, men and women are still bowing before idols on their own plain of Dura due to peer pressure.

Now, these three young men could have reasoned and rationalized, "Nebuchadnezzar has actually treated us pretty well. He has appointed us to positions of honor. He has empowered us by giving us a good education and well-paying jobs. If we don't bow, we will look pretty unappreciative. Furthermore, we're in Babylon—and, as they say, "When in Babylon, do as the Babylonians do.' Besides, in this situation, the end—staying alive—seems to justify the means." But there is not a single hint of this in their attitudes. They seem never to have entertained one of these thoughts. They had already decided which way they were going to turn when they eventually arrived at the intersection of Peer Pressure Corner.

When the Music Starts

But we digress. Back to the big event.

The band started to play, and everyone—thousands of people—all bowed down . . . except these three young men. They stood out like sore thumbs that day out there on the plain of Dura.

When the music starts and peer pressure mounts, we will respond in one of two ways. If we are choosing to love God and obey His Word, we will respond with *conviction*. But if what men say has become more important to us than what God says and we are controlled by the world, we will respond with *compromise*. Peer pressure compelled everyone to bow down. Most Babylonians just went along with the crowd. But three men stood tall and didn't bow. They were governed by an inner principle and were not going to give in to an outer pressure. They had learned an important life lesson: how to live with pressure.

As so many people do today, Shadrach, Meshach, and Abed-Nego could have said, "I may be bowing down on the outside, but I'm standing up on the inside!" or "We can't fight this system. We might as well join in just this once. God knows our heart. And, after all, what use would we be to Him if we were incinerated in the furnace?" Sadly, such compromise has replaced conviction in the vocabularies of many professed Christ-followers today.

In the moment it is so much easier to go along with the crowd. Being in the moral minority is definitely tough. Our faith community is loaded with opinions, but convictions seem to be missing. In fact, *conviction* has become a lost word in our Christian vocabulary.

Today's Idols

Of course, idols are not confined to some plain of Dura. They are all around us in our culture today. Many of us bow before the idols of possessions, projects, people, and pleasure. Could it be that some of us have come to the point where what other people think about us is more important to us than what God thinks about us? Framed as a more personal question, is what others are saying more important to you than what God is saying? The real tragedy today is that many people are so spiritually desensitized they are not even aware of pressures to stray from their faith.

Daniel's friends Shadrach, Meshach, and Abed-Nego teach us to live with the pressures of life that come our way. Our faith will be tested on our own plain of Dura, where *tolerance* is still the byword. We, too, will hear the band begin to play and watch as almost everyone around us bows down. Remember, you and I will have what we tolerate. In a culture advocating tolerance at all costs, we must learn to live with the pressure it exerts. In the final analysis, what God says is still much more important than what we may think or what anyone else might say about what we do or don't do.

10

LIVING WITH PRINCIPLE

Then Nebuchadnezzar, in rage and fury, gave the command to bring Shadrach, Meshach, and Abed-Nego. So they brought these men before the king. Nebuchadnezzar spoke, saying to them, "Is it true, Shadrach, Meshach, and Abed-Nego, that you do not serve my gods or worship the gold image which I have set up? Now if you are ready at the time you hear the sound of the horn, flute, harp, lyre, and psaltery, in symphony with all kinds of music, and you fall down and worship the image which I have made, good! But if you do not worship, you shall be cast immediately into the midst of a burning fiery furnace. And who is the god who will deliver you from my hands?"

Shadrach, Meshach, and Abed-Nego answered and said to the king, "O Nebuchadnezzar, we have no need to answer you in this matter."

—DANIEL 3:13–16

Ask our pluralistic American culture to identify the most intolerant group in our nation today, and in virtual unanimity the answer will be . . . evangelical Christians. In a myriad of not-so-subtle ways, this erroneous idea is being branded into the American psyche. Tolerance is the flag flown high in circles of influence, but Americans are taught to tolerate everyone except those who believe in absolute and biblical truth. Evangelicals counter by pointing out that one reason they are called "conservatives" is that they are trying to conserve things we have long held dear, such things as moral values, the Constitution, common decency, and religious freedom.

Advocates of today's tolerance love to quote the Bible. Their favorite verse is Matthew 7:1: "Judge not, that you be not judged." Unfortunately, they take it out of its context and fail to note that in the very next verse, we find that our Lord is really speaking here about self-righteousness, about setting ourselves up to judge others who may have a "speck" in their eye while we have a huge "beam" in our own that blinds us to all reality.

The Testing of Our Faith

We have just seen in the previous chapter how we must learn to live with peer pressure. We now arrive at the verses that teach us that choosing to live according to God's truth and biblical principles also has to do with *fear* pressure. Upon getting word that Shadrach, Meshach, and Abed-Nego refused to bow before his awesome image, Nebuchadnezzar—now enraged—called them into his presence. He could not believe what he had heard. The audacity of these three young men was hard for him to grasp. So that there would be no misunderstanding, Nebuchadnezzar afforded them another chance: they could bow . . . or they could burn. We are not talking about peer pressure here. This was fear pressure.

When fear comes knocking on our door, we respond to it—as we do to peer pressure—in one of two ways. If we are being governed by inner principles found in God's Word, we respond with courage. If we are being governed by pressure from the world's way of thinking, we will respond with cowardice. In light of this observation, listen to the declaration of these three brave young men: "Our God whom we serve is able to deliver us from the burning fiery furnace, and He will deliver us from your hand, O king. But if not, let it be known to you, O king, that we do not serve your gods, nor will we worship the gold image which you have set up" (Daniel 3:17–18). Shadrach, Meshach, and Abed-Nego responded with unbelievable courage.

Remember, these were not the young men's real names. Their Hebrew names were Hananiah, Mishael, and Azariah. But they tolerated the change to Babylonian names because there was no clear biblical command against such. They went along with the change in their language and the change in their literature for the same reasons. But, like their friend Daniel, they drew the line when it came to doing something contrary to the teachings of their Torah, their Bible. They well knew those words, written by God's own finger at Mount Sinai, that had been passed to Moses, who, in turn, recorded them for all posterity: "You shall have no other gods before Me. You shall not make for yourself a carved image—any likeness of anything that is in heaven above, or that is in the earth beneath, or that is in the water under the earth" (Exodus 20:3–4). I am sure they were also holding deep in their hearts Moses' other words in their holy book: "You shall remember that the LORD your God led you all the way these forty years in the wilderness, to humble you and test you, to know what was in your heart, whether you would keep His commandments or not" (Deuteronomy 8:2). God was testing Shadrach, Meshach, and Abed-Nego. Our own faith will be tested as well. If our enemy cannot get us to bow to peer pressure, he will seek to get us to bend under fear pressure.

"Is It True?"

Fear is what causes most of us to feel the real pressure to compromise and conform. There is the fear of losing our jobs if we do not step over the line just a little. More than a few young people have lost their virginity too early in life due to the fear of not being popular. Other people have a fear of being different and convince themselves that everyone else is stepping over the line or bowing down. But in the face of tremendous external pressure, these three young Hebrews possessed inner principle and stood firm and tall despite the king's death threats. Shadrach, Meshach, and Abed-Nego made it clear that some things are nonnegotiable.

Nebuchadnezzar looked them straight in the eye and asked, "Is it true?" (Daniel 3:14). That pointed question is pertinent to us as well. We ought to be asking it of ourselves: *Is it true?* The world around us, like Nebuchadnezzar of old, wants to know, "Is it true?" Or are our convictions just something we *profess* but don't really *possess*? What about you? You claim to be a follower of Christ. Is it really true? Really?

The Higher Law

This encounter between Nebuchadnezzar and Shadrach, Meshach, and Abed-Nego brings us face-to-face with an issue that many will have to decide about in coming days. I am speaking here about civil disobedience. What are we to do when our king makes a decree that runs counter to our deep convictions rooted in God's Word and His commandments? After all, our Lord admonished us strongly to be subject to those governmental authorities that rule over us. The apostle Paul was clear: everyone should "be subject to the governing authorities" (Romans 13:1). Peter, the head of the Jerusalem church, weighed in here as well: "Submit yourselves to every ordinance of man for the Lord's sake, whether to the king as supreme, or to governors" (1 Peter 2:13–14). Is it ever appropriate for believers to disobey civil authority? Yes—but where do we draw the line?

The Bible gives clear direction about civil disobedience: we are compelled to disobey civil law when it is in direct opposition to God's laws set out in Scripture. One such occurrence took place in Egypt and is recorded in Exodus 1. Civil law—the Pharaoh's edict—called for the Hebrew midwives to destroy the lives of all Hebrew boys at their birth, but that was in direct contrast to all the Bible says about the gift of life. So the midwives disobeyed: they delivered the Hebrews babies and protected them. Here in Daniel 3 we find our Hebrew friends refusing to obey a directive that was diametrically opposed to the laws of God. We also see in the book of Acts that when the early believers were instructed to cease preaching in the name of Jesus, they replied, "We ought to obey God rather than men" (Acts 5:29).

There is a common thread woven through every one of these events. In each situation, there is a direct conflict between man's law and God's law, and the believers were willing to suffer the consequences of their civil disobedience. As believers, we have the biblical responsibility to submit to and support governmental authority. After all, its authority issues forth from God Himself. Our observance of the law is a positive public testimony of our faith. It is the right thing to do unless civil law directly contradicts God's law. Then, like the early believers in Jerusalem, we should "obey God rather than men" and face the consequences as those early believers so bravely did before us.

In this world that is increasingly advocating tolerance at all costs, we must learn to live with pressure and be guided by inner principles we get from the Bible. Before this week is out, we will most likely—at some place and in some way—find ourselves out there on the plain of Dura or standing before the king. Scripture demands that—like Shadrach, Meshach, and Abed-Nego—we be governed by that inner principle that empowers us to respond with courage and conviction, not cowardice and compromise.

After all, our world is asking, "Is it true?"

11

LIVING WITH PERSPECTIVE

Shadrach, Meshach, and Abed-Nego answered and said to the king . . . "Our God whom we serve is able to deliver us from the burning fiery furnace, and He will deliver us from your hand, O king. But if not, let it be known to you, O king, that we do not serve your gods, nor will we worship the gold image which you have set up."

—DANIEL 3:16–18

*I*n a world increasingly hostile to biblical values, it is as important for us to keep a proper perspective on its ungodly ways as it is to learn to live with unbiblical pressure and according to biblical principle. When confronted by the king about their actions, Shadrach, Meshach, and Abed-Nego had an immediate reply ready. They didn't have to think about their options. Their response to the king's inquiry revealed their amazing perspective on their situation. And all of us would do well to incorporate it and emulate it. Let's dissect the young Hebrews' perspective.

"OUR GOD WHOM WE SERVE"

Shadrach, Meshach, and Abed-Nego began by saying, "Our God" (Daniel 3:17). Do you sense their camaraderie here?

They were going through this together. They were standing together not just out there on the plain facing immense peer pressure, but also now, before the king and under what must have been incredible fear pressure to give in and go along. These young men were teaching us how much we, in our own tolerant culture, need each other in our own day-to-day challenges and particularly in raising our children in such a world system. We need to live with this perspective: He is not just *my* God; He is *our* God. We need each other.

Shadrach, Meshach, and Abed-Nego continued, "Our God *whom we serve*." A lot of people in our day can say "our God," but can they repeat the phrase "whom we serve"? As a pastor for decades, I watched more than a few men and women who professed Christ, but when it came to truly serving Him, came up a bit short. Then, when the crisis came, they so often faced it with cowardice and joined the others bowing down out on the plain. On the other hand, I have had the opportunity to watch people who served God faithfully in many ways come to a crisis where their faith was severely tested, and I watched as they faced the moment with courage. Learning to live with perspective is not simply something we say, but it is also something we do.

He Is Able

These young Hebrews had the confident perspective that this God they were serving was "able to deliver" them (Daniel 3:17). This was not some superficial speculation on their part, but a solid conviction based on the Word of God. These men knew the Word and staked their lives on it. They truly believed that their God was, indeed, able to do anything, anywhere, anytime. After all, this is the real issue, isn't it? God *is* able. When we have this settled in our minds and begin to live with this perspective, we will have no problem out on our plain of Dura or even if we find ourselves standing in the king's presence.

Whatever your need . . . *God is able*. Think about it. If you are in need of grace, "God is able to make all grace abound toward you" (2 Corinthians 9:8). If there is some temptation knocking at your door, "He Himself has suffered, being tempted, [so] He is able to aid those who are tempted" (Hebrews 2:18). Are you in need of assurance of salvation? "He is . . . able to save to the uttermost those who come to God through Him" (Hebrews 7:25). Are you needing security? Paul said, "I know whom I have believed and am persuaded that He is able to keep what I have committed to Him until that Day" (2 Timothy 1:12). We all are in need of strength to keep going in difficult days: "[He] is able to keep you from stumbling, and to present you faultless before the presence of His glory with exceeding joy" (Jude v. 24). One thing is certain in these days of uncertainty: God is able! Fill in the blank with one of your concerns: "Our God whom I serve is able to _____." And He is!

"BUT IF NOT!"

The real secret of Shadrach, Meshach, and Abed-Nego's positive perspective is found in three little words recorded for all posterity in Daniel 3:18: "But if not . . ." They boldly declared to Nebuchadnezzar, "But if not, let it be known to you, O king, that we do not serve your gods, nor will we worship the gold image which you have set up." The object of their faith was not God's performance. It was their Lord and Him alone. Many profess faith as long as they have the blessings or the feeling or some other trinket to hold on to. Shadrach and his two friends, however, had placed their faith in God and God alone, not in what they could get from Him.

We, too, must maintain this perspective and say in the face of the many things that come our way, "Yes, God is able to deliver us—but if not . . . !" Some of us will have to say this in the face of sickness: "He is able to deliver us—but if not . . ." Some may need these words in the face of business failures: "He is able to deliver us—but if not . . ." We may need to say this in times of frustration or even defeat: "He is able to deliver us—but if not . . ." There are times when we pray but do not see the answer, and we need this perspective: "He is able to deliver us—but if not . . ." The issue is never God's ability. He is always able! The issue is His sovereign will.

Now, some believers live with the idea that if they are delivered from some furnace of life, everyone should join in the celebration. *But if not . . .* if they are not delivered from that furnace, then they should quietly find a place to hide so as not to do damage to God's reputation. What kind of God do they serve? The same God who gave so much to Job also took so much from him. The same God who miraculously delivered Simon Peter from prison allowed James to be martyred by Herod's sword. The very same God who allowed John the Baptist to be decapitated delivered others in similar circumstances and situations. This needed perspective is closely akin to what Job said: "[Even] though He slay me, yet will I trust Him" (Job 13:15). This was also the positive perspective of Esther's classic pronouncement, "If I perish, I perish" (Esther 4:16).

When these three brave young men stood before the king saying, "But if not . . . ," they demonstrated for all of us who would come after them a level of mature faith. Look at this perspective. Whether or not God delivers us from the furnace should never change our conviction that He *is* able. If anyone claims to have lost their faith due to a situation when God did not come through as they thought He should, their complaint is proof that theirs was a faith built only upon performance. We all know people who have dropped out of the race because even though they said, "Our God whom we serve is able," they could not add those three little words *but if not. . . .* Can you?

DID YOU NOTICE?

We should find it interesting here that Shadrach, Meshach, and Abed-Nego, faced with a life-threatening situation, never asked God to deliver them. They simply threw themselves upon Him and His sovereign will for their lives and—come what may—they would praise Him. It is one thing to stand tall and confident in the Lord on the day of faith's victory, but quite another to stand on the day of faith's testings and trials.

We all want to walk across the stage and receive a diploma, but not everyone is willing to pay the price of multiple tests, hard study, term papers, and final exams.

First, our Hebrew friends would not bow to peer pressure. They will not bend beneath fear pressure. Their victory was not won in the fiery furnace, but right here, before the king, living under pressure, on principle, and with perspective. Once we are in a fiery furnace, it's too late to decide what we will say or what we will do.

In a world advocating tolerance at all costs, we must learn to live with pressures that come our way. We must learn to live with godly inner principles embedded deep in our very being. And, above all, we need to learn to live with perspective: "Our God whom we serve is able to deliver us—but if not . . . !"

12

LIVING WITH PROTECTION

Then Nebuchadnezzar was furious with Shadrach, Meshach and Abednego, and his attitude toward them changed. He ordered the furnace heated seven times hotter than usual and commanded some of the strongest soldiers in his army to tie up Shadrach, Meshach and Abednego and throw them into the blazing furnace. So these men, wearing their robes, trousers, turbans and other clothes, were bound and thrown into the blazing furnace. The king's command was so urgent and the furnace so hot that the flames of the fire killed the soldiers who took up Shadrach, Meshach and Abednego, and these three men, firmly tied, fell into the blazing furnace.

Then King Nebuchadnezzar leaped to his feet in amazement and asked his advisers, "Weren't there three men that we tied up and threw into the fire?" They replied, "Certainly, Your Majesty."

He said, "Look! I see four men walking around in the fire, unbound and unharmed, and the fourth looks like a son of the gods."

Nebuchadnezzar then approached the opening of the blazing furnace and shouted, "Shadrach, Meshach and Abednego, servants of the Most High God, come out! Come here!"

So Shadrach, Meshach and Abednego came out of the

fire, and the satraps, prefects, governors and royal advisers crowded around them. They saw that the fire had not harmed their bodies, nor was a hair of their heads singed; their robes were not scorched, and there was no smell of fire on them.

Then Nebuchadnezzar said, "Praise be to the God of Shadrach, Meshach and Abednego, who has sent his angel and rescued his servants! They trusted in him and defied the king's command and were willing to give up their lives rather than serve or worship any god except their own God. Therefore I decree that the people of any nation or language who say anything against the God of Shadrach, Meshach and Abednego be cut into pieces and their houses be turned into piles of rubble, for no other god can save in this way."

Then the king promoted Shadrach, Meshach and Abednego in the province of Babylon.

—DANIEL 3:19–30 NIV

We now find our three Hebrew friends in a hot spot: Shadrach, Meshach, and Abed-Nego were "bound . . . and [ready to be] cast into the midst of the burning fiery furnace" (Daniel 3:21). No one escaped such a horrible fate at this point. There was nowhere to go. There was no way out. They seemed doomed to meet an indescribably painful death. Yet they have one final lesson to teach those of us who are seeking to find our way in a culture that, much like theirs, has lost its way. We, too, can learn to stand strong for what we believe in even if it's at great cost.

God allowed Shadrach, Meshach, and Abed-Nego to be cast into the fiery furnace, and that experience, although difficult to endure, actually resulted in their own good. They had been stripped of everything except one thing: knowledge of their God. And I like to think they were standing on a promise of God found in the writings of the prophet Isaiah, writings they had known back in Israel: "When you walk through the fire, you shall not be burned, nor shall the flame scorch you" (Isaiah 43:2).

God certainly could have delivered the young men from the fiery furnace. After all, He delivered Israel from sure defeat and death at the hands of the pursuing Egyptians by parting the Red Sea for their passage toward the promised land. When the people of Israel wandered in the wilderness, He delivered them from starvation by miraculously providing manna from heaven every day. Yes, God could have delivered Shadrach, Meshach, and Abed-Nego from the fiery furnace, but He had a better plan. Deliverance *from* the furnace was not nearly as significant as deliverance *from within* the fiery furnace. Could it be that some of us have missed God's plan and purpose because we got mad when He didn't deliver us *from* our own fiery experience of life? He hasn't forgotten a single one of us. It just might be that His plan for you is a deliverance *from within* the furnace that will result in your good and His glory.

Consequences of Commitment

None of us should think that because we are Christ-followers, we are immune to the various trials of life. Jesus Himself told us that the rain falls on the just and the unjust alike (Matthew 5:45). He also specifically warned us, His followers, that we would experience troubles in this life (John 16:33). Ask the apostle Paul if he was immune to life's challenges and trials: he was stoned at Lystra and left for dead, and he spoke of a "thorn in the flesh" that continually tormented and agitated him (2 Corinthians 12:7). Ask Simon Peter if his position in Christ's inner circle left him immune to trials of life: tradition says he ended up being crucified . . . upside down. Ask those in the roll call of the faithful listed in Hebrews 11 if they were immune to difficulties: some were stoned, and others were even cut in half. These were all people, like you and me, who made up their minds to live out in faith the "but if nots" of life.

No doubt many reading these words find themselves either about to be thrown into some furnace of life or already in one with the heat being turned up. Know that some of our trials come for the sake of *prevention*. Paul said, "Lest I should be exalted above measure by the abundance of the revelations, a thorn in the flesh was given to me" (2 Corinthians 12:7). Some trials come our way for *proof* of our faith. In the midst of his own pain and suffering, Job said, "I have heard of You by the hearing of the ear, but now my eye sees You" (Job 42:5). And trials often come our way for our own *profit.* The writer of Hebrews relates that our "human fathers indeed for a few days chastened us as seemed best to them, but He for our profit, that we may be partakers of His holiness" (12:9–10).

So, through the lens of Daniel 3, take a good look at Shadrach, Meshach, and Abed-Nego in the fiery furnace. What happens when we do not bow in compromise and do not bend in cowardice? We do not burn! Nebuchadnezzar came to look into the furnace and was startled. He exclaimed, "Look! I see four men loose, walking in the midst of the fire; and they are not hurt, and the form of the fourth is like the Son of God" (Daniel 3:25). This statement brings us to a brief aside for a quick math lesson. How many went into the fiery furnace? Three. How many did the king see when he peered into the furnace? Four. How many came out of the furnace? Three. What does this tell us? Our Lord is always with us. If any of us find ourselves in a fiery-furnace experience and look around closely, we will find Him . . . right there . . . with us. We are never alone.

THE BLESSINGS OF FIRES

The fiery furnace resulted in good for Shadrach, Meshach, and Abed-Nego. The Bible records that their bonds were "loose[d]" (Daniel 3:25). Maybe the Fourth Person untied them, or maybe the fire burned away that which had them bound up. Often we, too, find that the flames of our own uncomfortable experience have their way of freeing us from so many things that bind us. I have watched men bound in ropes of pride go through a furnace experience of life that ended in their good as those very things that tied them up were loosed forever. The fiery furnace turned out to be for their good . . . and it will ours also.

Not only did Shadrach, Meshach, and Abed-Nego find *freedom* in the fires, but they found *fellowship* as well. That Fourth Man was the Lord Himself. He stepped from His throne of glory and came down to walk through the fire with these three young men who had stood so tall for Him. And Jesus will do the same for you! Don't quit in your own time of testing. Look around right now. He is in there with you. You are not alone. God never promised to keep us out of the fiery furnace, but He did show us that He would get in it with us and bring us out without a hair singed and without the smell of smoke on us.

But the story of our Hebrew friends doesn't end just yet. Their trust in their God was a powerful testimony to the king. Listen to him: "Blessed be the God of Shadrach, Meshach, and Abed-Nego, who sent His Angel and delivered His servants who trusted in Him" (Daniel 3:28). Even a world advocating tolerance on every front stops and takes note when God shows up. Nebuchadnezzar continued, "There is no other God who can deliver like this" (v. 29). This is the very point Peter was driving home in the New Testament when he said, "In this you greatly rejoice, though now for a little while, if need be, you have been grieved by various trials, that the genuineness of your faith, being much more precious than gold that perishes, though it is tested by fire, *may be found to praise, honor and glory at the revelation of Jesus Christ"* (1 Peter 1:6–7, emphasis added).

God can do amazing reversals! The king promoted the three young men, and this same man who had demanded that all the people bow down and worship the image he built now bowed before the King over all other kings. Solomon's wise words are still true: "When a man's ways please the LORD, He makes even his enemies to be at peace with him" (Proverbs 16:7).

MAY WE . . .

What have we learned from this trip out to the plain of Dura and into the fiery furnace? God is in control. His finger is on the thermostat. And guess what? He still would have been in control had He allowed Shadrach, Meshach, and Abed-Nego to perish in the flames. Yes, "Our God whom we serve is able to deliver us—but if not . . . !" And if not, He is still God, and He is still good.

Jack Evans had it right when he said, "You have what you tolerate." We are living in a world where tolerance has become the new law of the land. "All truth claims, value propositions, and lifestyles are equally valid" is the constant theme of our day. But we can learn to live with *pressure*. Shadrach, Meshach, and Abed-Nego did, and so can we. We can learn to live according to God's *principles*. In fact, we must if we intend to survive and pass on to our kids and grandkids His truth and His values. Above all, we can learn to live with the *perspective* that our sovereign God can deliver us and with that "but if not" attitude. And when we find ourselves in a hot spot, we can learn to live with His *protection*. The furnace is for our good and for God's glory.

Yes, when all is said and done . . . you have what you tolerate! And the result is a world of challenges for God's people.

SECTION IV

ON A SEARCH FOR SIGNIFICANCE

*T*here is an amazing transition taking place in a segment of the American population. The past years have seen a significant number of middle-aged adults on a quest to move from success to significance. This particular generation has acquired more possessions, position, and power than any in history. It set its sights on achieving success and, for the most part, hit the bull's-eye. But that success has done little to fill the emptiness of the human heart. Sadly, this successful generation also leads all others in such things as divorce, suicide, addictions, and loneliness.

This unsatisfying success has brought about a search . . . a search for meaning in life, a search for some semblance of significance. By no means is this search something new. As we come now to Daniel 4, we find one of the most successful men in all recorded history: King Nebuchadnezzar now steps to center stage. He had achieved more power and wealth, accompanied by all that goes along with those things, than most people dream about in their wildest imaginations. We are about to observe his own personal journey from success to significance when he came to the ultimate conclusion that "the Most High rules in the kingdom of men" (v. 17).

The Way Up

One of the problems of our Western culture today is that too many people still believe significance exists in direct proportion to one's perceived successes in life. Most of us are still looking for significance in all the wrong places. We think, perhaps subconsciously, that if we just work harder and do better than anyone else, we will find significance in life. So we focus on selling more policies or products, getting a bigger home in a better neighborhood, driving a fancier car, getting our kids into the best schools, doing anything that builds bigger kingdoms for ourselves.

Our culture has been permeated by this success syndrome for decades now. Look in the bookstores. Those books on the top shelf teach you to become the greatest. They tell you, "The way up . . . is *up*! Promote yourself. Think positive. You are the best!" But we are about to see that Nebuchadnezzar is exhibit A of the fallacy of this philosophy. In fact, his story is recorded here in Daniel for all posterity to see that, in reality, the way up is actually down!

A thousand voices in our culture have been telling us in a thousand ways to build up our self-confidence, but the Bible is telling us to "have no confidence in the flesh" (Philippians 3:3). Our culture says, "Don't be afraid to promote yourself," but the Bible says quite the opposite. It instructs us to crucify ourselves, to die to self (Galatians 2:20). The culture shouts at us, "You must increase!" but John the Baptist's words still echo down through the centuries: "He must increase, but

I must decrease" (John 3:30). The culture also proclaims: "Never be satisfied with what you have or where you are." These words are heard in a multitude of motivational meetings. But the Bible still instructs us through the words of Paul to learn, in "whatever state I am, to be content" (Philippians 4:11). Our culture is cheering, "You're number one! You're number one!" while our Bible calls us to humble ourselves "under the mighty hand of God" (1 Peter 5:6).

SUCCESS OR SIGNIFICANCE?

What about you? Are you on a search for success . . . or a search for significance? As the verses of Daniel 4 are about to unfold before us, we see an amazing transformation in King Nebuchadnezzar. Listen to him as he pounds his chest and boasts, "Is not this great Babylon, that I have built for a royal dwelling by my mighty power and for the honor of my majesty?" (Daniel 4:30). Those are the words of a man standing in the spotlight, consumed with his own self-importance and success. But a few verses later, listen to the proof of his startling transformation from success to significance: "Now, I, Nebuchadnezzar, praise and extol and honor the King of heaven, all of whose works are truth, and His ways justice. And those who walk in pride He is able to put down" (v. 37). What happened?

Those are actually the last words of one of the most ingenious and innovative, powerful and productive men who ever lived. He left us a lasting legacy. He not only passed from success to significance in this one chapter, but he left us his own story to show us the way to this invaluable discovery in life—that the way down is up and the way up is down.

Like Nebuchadnezzar, we, too, have that same choice. We can base our self-worth on our success and our ability to achieve goals and acquire stuff in life so that others take notice. Or we can base our sense of worth on significance that is only found in the place this king found his: in our identity in the Lord Himself, who set us apart since we were in our mother's womb for a purpose that no one can fulfill quite like we can. Now, that's significance!

As we have been unlocking the Daniel Code to learn to live in a culture that is losing its way, we have heard from Daniel and from his three friends, Shadrach, Meshach, and Abed-Nego. Now it is time to hear from the king himself. He has an extraordinary testimony to share. He knows all too well from personal experience the way to move from success to significance. He has two simple things to say to us: the way down is up, and the way up is down!

13   THE WAY DOWN IS UP

The king spoke, saying, "Is not this great Babylon, that I have built for a royal dwelling by my mighty power and for the honor of my majesty?"

—DANIEL 4:30

Most of our culture does not believe it, but it is eventually proved true: the way down is up. Most think the way up is up. That is, if you want to scale the ladder of success, you must have a strong element of self-promotion about whatever you do and say. But our Lord's words in Matthew 23:12 are still true: "Whoever exalts himself will be humbled." This was His way of saying, "The way down is up."

Nebuchadnezzar was a man geared and governed, moved and motivated by the success syndrome for most of his life. The more he had, the more he craved. He had built a nine-story golden image in his prideful desire to be recognized and worshiped. Ruled by pride, he—like some people today—had convinced himself that the way up was up. Until, that is, he had a confrontation with the living God.

STARTING WITH THE ENDING

The introduction to Daniel 4 is, in fact, its conclusion:

Nebuchadnezzar the king, to all peoples, nations, and languages that dwell in all the earth:

Peace be multiplied to you.

I thought it good to declare the signs and wonders that the Most High God has worked for me.

How great are His signs, and how mighty His wonders!

His kingdom is an everlasting kingdom,

And His dominion is from generation to generation.

(vv. 1–3)

These introductory words actually come *after* Nebuchadnezzar's humiliating and humbling ordeal recorded in chapter 4. The same man who once brutally ravished nations with an iron hand now said, "Peace be multiplied to you" (v. 1). This is the same man who had conquered nation after nation, slaughtering untold multitudes of people, uprooting entire families, and taking hostage millions of slaves for the express purpose of building his golden city of Babylon, all to feed his massive ego. This is the same man who, in Daniel 3, had, in a rage, heated the furnace seven times hotter than normal for the three Hebrew young men who refused to worship at the statue. This is the same man spoken of in 2 Kings 25 who slew King Zedekiah's sons right in front of him and then put out Zedekiah's eyes so that the last thing he ever saw was the brutal death of his own boys. In his quest for success at all costs, Nebuchadnezzar stepped on anyone and everyone in his path. He thought the way up was up. But now? Now Nebuchadnezzar spoke of peace.

What happened? On his journey from success to significance, Nebuchadnezzar had to learn his lessons the hard way. Now he not only was speaking of peace, but He was giving credit where credit was rightfully due. Listen to him: "I thought it good to declare the signs and wonders that the Most High God has worked for me" (Daniel 4:2). Nebuchadnezzar had made a remarkable admission: the kingdoms of men are only temporary. One rises, then falls . . . always. But God is in ultimate control, and it is only His kingdom that is an everlasting kingdom. And, furthermore, this once-prideful king wanted the whole world to know what God had done for him.

How could this transition from success to significance have possibly happened to this person of such position and privilege? It begins with this admission: "I, Nebuchadnezzar, was at rest in my house and flourishing in my palace" (Daniel 4:4). Look at him. He had it made; he had no worries; he was "at rest." And, if that were not enough, he was "flourishing." He was at the apex of success in the world's eyes. I can almost see him, feet propped up on his desk, leaning back in his leather chair, thinking, *I have it made now.* Then he dozed off and had a dream. This one frightened him. He saw a tree that had grown tall and strong and that spread its branches in a wide circumference. It was an awesome sight. But as he watched, it was cut down and hauled off! The stump of the tree was all that remained. He looked closer, and a band of iron and brass kept the stump from being completely uprooted.

Deeply troubled, Nebuchadnezzar once again needed someone to interpret a dream for him. So he called in the same type of losers who had failed him in the past. (A man ruled by prideful ambition and worldly success never learns.) It was no surprise that not a one of them could interpret the dream.

ANOTHER DREAM INTERPRETED

Daniel once more came to the rescue, and he had some good news and some bad news for the king. The good news was that Nebuchadnezzar was great and strong like the mighty tree in the dream. But then came the bad news: he was going to be cut down. And so there would be no doubt, Daniel was blunt: "The tree that you saw . . . it is you, O king, who have grown and become strong" (Daniel 4:20–22).

Daniel saw that this mighty tree would fall; however, it would not die. This dream went on to describe a man who would lose all reason and, for a period of time, even behave like an animal. He would be driven from men, and his "dwelling shall be with the beasts of the field, and they shall make you eat grass like oxen" (Daniel 4:25). Daniel prophesied that the king was about to temporarily lose his mind. He would go through a period of insanity, after which he would be restored to his right mind and to his kingdom as well. Nebuchadnezzar was about to find out the hard way that the way down is up. Nebuchadnezzar had climbed the ladder of success—only to come crashing down; he went down by going up. Yes, "the Most High rules in the kingdom of men" (v. 25).

God has His own ways of moving some of us from success to significance. The kingdoms of men all rise and all fall, but the Most High still rules over every single one of them.

Daniel now began to passionately plead with Nebuchadnezzar: "O King, let my advice be acceptable to you; break off your sins by being righteous, and your iniquities by showing mercy to the poor. Perhaps there may be a lengthening of your prosperity" (Daniel 4:27). Daniel also warned the king that if he would not break from his sin, he would be broken by that sin. But pride has its way of getting in the way of wise counsel. Our own culture has witnessed countless broken and wasted lives of men and women who stubbornly refused to break away from their sin.

WARNING HEEDED?

By the world's standards, no one was more successful than King Nebuchadnezzar, but it was a success virtually void of significance. He chose sinful conceit—keeping his eyes on himself instead of on God—rather than finding significance in acknowledging and serving God. It is so much better to break from our sins than to be broken by our sins. Just ask this king. He was about to encounter the truth that "the Most High rules over the kingdoms of men." Nebuchadnezzar's experience is a stark warning to anyone in our contemporary culture caught up in the success syndrome and thinking that the way up is really up. For any of us who are right now doing whatever is necessary to become successful, Daniel's warning is as relevant and vital as it was to an ancient Babylonian king: "Break off your sins" (Daniel 4:27).

Judgment didn't fall on King Nebuchadnezzar all at once. It seldom ever does. Twelve months passed. God extended His grace for an entire year. But the king did nothing in response. In fact, he kept strutting around the roof of his palace like a proud peacock, saying, "Is not this the great Babylon, that I have built for a royal dwelling by my mighty power and for the honor of my majesty?" (Daniel 4:30).

Then, swiftly and suddenly, judgment came—and it came when the king least expected it. He found out the hard way that the way down is up. "While the word was still in the king's mouth, a voice fell from heaven: 'King Nebuchadnezzar, to you it is spoken: the kingdom has departed from you!'" (Daniel 4:31). Since the king would not break from his sin, we now find him broken by it. Nebuchadnezzar's own testimony should be a stark warning to all of us in our success-crazed culture: "Those who walk in pride, [God] is able to put down" (v. 37). Nebuchadnezzar had thought the way up was up. But he was dead wrong.

It is still true—and it always will be true: "Whoever exalts himself will be humbled, and whoever humbles himself will be exalted" (Matthew 23:12). The way down is up! And the way up is down!

THE WAY UP IS DOWN

Part 1

While the word was still in the king's mouth, a voice fell from heaven: "King Nebuchadnezzar, to you it is spoken: the kingdom has departed from you! And they shall drive you from men, and your dwelling shall be with the beasts of the field. They shall make you eat grass like oxen; and seven times shall pass over you, until you know that the Most High rules in the kingdom of men, and gives it to whomever He chooses."

That very hour the word was fulfilled concerning Nebuchadnezzar; he was driven from men and ate grass like oxen; his body was wet with the dew of heaven till his hair had grown like eagles' feathers and his nails like birds' claws.

And at the end of the time I, Nebuchadnezzar, lifted my eyes to heaven, and my understanding returned to me; and I blessed the Most High and praised and honored Him who lives forever:

> *For His dominion is an everlasting dominion,*
> *And His kingdom is from generation to generation.*
> *All the inhabitants of the earth are reputed as nothing;*

He does according to His will in the army of
   heaven
And among the inhabitants of the earth.
No one can restrain His hand
Or say to Him, "What have You done?"

At the same time my reason returned to me, and for the glory of my kingdom, my honor and splendor returned to me. My counselors and nobles resorted to me, I was restored to my kingdom, and excellent majesty was added to me. Now I, Nebuchadnezzar, praise and extol and honor the King of heaven, all of whose works are truth, and His ways justice. And those who walk in pride He is able to put down.

—DANIEL 4:31–37

*S*uccess says, "Is not this great Babylon, that I have built for a royal dwelling by my mighty power and for the honor of my majesty?" (Daniel 4:30). Those possessed by the success syndrome fill their speech with possessive personal pronouns. Their lives are all about *me, me, me . . . my, my, my . . . I, I, I*. Significance, on the other hand, says, "I, Nebuchadnezzar, lifted my eyes to heaven, and my understanding returned to me; and I blessed the Most High and praised and honored Him who lives forever . . . all of whose works are truth, and His ways justice. And those who walk in pride He is able to put down" (vv. 34–37). This is Nebuchadnezzar's way of telling us that, in the final analysis, the only real way up is down. Only people who truly humble themselves will be lifted up.

True success in life always and only comes after we pass through the door of significance, of understanding who we are in God's eyes. As I previously noted in *The James Code: 52 Scripture Principles for Putting Your Faith into Action*, the New Testament writer James reminded us of this truth by bluntly stating, "God resists the proud" (James 4:6). He chose a Greek word to translate as "resist," and that Greek word means "to battle against or to oppose forcefully." It is a military term. This is to say, God is set against those who are proud, and He has His own ways of taking a firm stand against them. On this journey toward significance in life, we find the way up is really down.

PRIDE SPOKEN

The Daniel 4 narrative opens with the king stepping onto his rooftop and looking far and wide over the magnificent city he had built. Its walls were eight stories high and forty feet across, and they extended for a total circumference of fifteen miles. Within those walls were fifty temples, one of which—shaped in the form of a pyramid—stood six hundred feet high with a statue atop extending another fifty feet toward the heavens. Everywhere Nebuchadnezzar looked, he saw fabulous palaces and gorgeous hanging gardens. The beautiful Euphrates River wound its way through the interior of the city. It must have been quite a sight to behold. As Nebuchadnezzar gazed over it, he proudly proclaimed, "Is not this great Babylon, that I have built for a royal dwelling by my mighty power and for the honor of my majesty?" (Daniel 4:30).

This very attitude still raises its ugly head all too often in our contemporary culture. Many people seem to think they really are in total control and running their own lives. In their own way, they stand on their rooftops and repeat Nebuchadnezzar's prideful proclamation.

Just one chapter earlier this same Nebuchadnezzar had watched in awe as God delivered the three Hebrew young men from the burning fiery furnace. He stood there and proclaimed, "Blessed be the God of Shadrach, Meshach, and Abed-Nego, who sent His Angel and delivered His servants. . . . There is no other God who can deliver like this" (Daniel 3:28–29). But that was yesterday, and talk is cheap. The king forgot all that and went his way unchanged . . . like so many of us are prone to do in the aftermath of some great victory God gives us.

As the king stood on his rooftop boasting of his greatness to himself and anyone within earshot, his demise came suddenly: "While the word was still in the king's mouth, a voice fell from heaven: . . . 'The kingdom has departed from you!'" (Daniel 4:31). Nebuchadnezzar had built a great wall. He had completely shut out all his enemies. He was at rest. He was flourishing. He was prancing around the palace in pomp and pride. He had shut everyone out—except the Lord God, who "rules in the kingdom of men" (v. 32).

Pride Judged

And so God's judgment fell swiftly on Nebuchadnezzar. It had to be horrible to watch. This once-proud king lost his mind. He ended up in such a state that he was actually walking around on all fours and eating grass like an animal. Earlier he was clothed in regal robes; now he wallowed in insanity, unkempt and uncontrollable. His hair became matted, and his fingernails grew long and thick, "like birds' claws" (Daniel 4:33).

This transformation happened suddenly—but not unexpectedly—as Nebuchadnezzar delivered his discourse about his dominance. God warns us for months, sometimes years. He gives us time to repent. But then, suddenly, judgment falls. Solomon acknowledged this truth: "He who is often rebuked, and hardens his neck, will *suddenly* be destroyed, and that, without remedy" (Proverbs 29:1, emphasis added). This is the way it happens: when we least expect it. Nebuchadnezzar exemplified the biblical truth: "Pride goes before destruction, and a haughty spirit before a fall" (Proverbs 16:18). God's grace had been extended to Nebuchadnezzar for many months, but, like so many of us, he did nothing in response. His experience should serve as a dire warning to all of us.

It was such pride that caused Lucifer, the angel of light, to be cast out of heaven (see Isaiah 14:12–15). It was pride that caused Adam and Eve to fall out of favor in Eden's garden. And it is this same pride that causes men and women in our contemporary culture—who, like Nebuchadnezzar, think they are indestructible—to find out the hard way that the way down is up.

Pride Replaced

But there is good news. The mighty, matchless monarch gets a second chance. The one who had conquered his known world now humbled himself (Daniel 4:34–37). The old arrogance was now gone. The old egotistical pride had vanished. What a scene it was as he now humbled himself before the true King of all kings. The arrogance expressed in Daniel 4:30 was now replaced by the adoration of verse 34: "I, Nebuchadnezzar, lifted my eyes to heaven, and my understanding returned to me; and I blessed the Most High and praised and honored Him who lives forever." These verbs indicate a continuous action: this attitude continued. It became the lifestyle for King Nebuchadnezzar going forward. He continued to bless God, to praise and honor Him, for the remainder of his days. Pride was replaced with praise; ego with exaltation; hubris with humility. He summed it up with his own words: "I, Nebuchadnezzar, praise and extol and honor the King of heaven, all of whose words are truth, and His ways justice. And, those who walk in pride He is able to put down" (v. 37). It was his way of saying, "The way up is really down!"

On his own journey to significance, the first thing King Nebuchadnezzar did was to lift his eyes to heaven (Daniel 4:34). Our own crisis experience in life can point us to God if we will allow it to do so. The psalmist of Israel framed it for all of us: "Before I was afflicted I went astray, but now I keep Your word. You are good, and do good; teach me Your statutes" (Psalm 119:67–68).

Yes, the way up is down.

15   THE WAY UP IS DOWN

Part 2

*N*ebuchadnezzar, the once-prideful potentate, had been restored: his reason was restored; his reputation was restored; his reign was restored. "I was restored to my kingdom, and excellent majesty was added to me" (Daniel 4:36). God keeps His promises. Daniel had reminded the king that in his dream the "tree" would not be completely destroyed. The stump and roots would remain, signifying that "your kingdom shall be [restored] to you, after you come to know that Heaven rules" (v. 26). God is faithful to His word . . . always and in all ways.

Hear King Nebuchadnezzar's last words: "Now I, Nebuchadnezzar, praise and extol and honor the King of heaven, all of whose works are truth, and His ways justice. And those who walk in pride He is able to put down" (Daniel 4:37). The curtain falls. That is it. We never hear from Nebuchadnezzar again, but he left us a legacy: this king showed us that "those who walk in pride [God] is able to put down." In other words, Nebuchadnezzar showed us that the way down is up, but the good news is . . . the way up is down!

The Potter and the Clay

The search for significance is one of the most basic pursuits of life, exceeding even the quest for money or pleasure. We are all on this search whether we realize it or not. Some of us have confused this search with the search for success. But deep within all of us is a desire for significance. It is the search of every human heart.

The Bible reveals that we were designed to be people of significance. We were created by God Himself. We are not just some random-chance occurrence in a larger evolutionary process. This desire within us for some semblance of significance is in our DNA. No one else on this planet, no one else who has ever lived, has a DNA exactly like yours. You are an individual, indescribably valuable to God. Significance comes in living life rooted in that truth; significance is enhanced when you find the job that no one can do quite like you can. Many attempts to gain significance in life today are futile because many are searching in all the wrong places. Genuine, fulfilling significance is found in God. And only in God.

We human beings haven't always been on this search. In fact, we were originally created with a sense of significance. The Bible says, "The LORD God formed man of the dust of the ground, and breathed into his nostrils the breath of life; and man became a living being" (Genesis 2:7). God created man differently than the rest of His creations. Before creating man, He had been busy with what we call *fiat* creation.

That is, God simply spoke, and it was so. With a spoken word, He spoke the world and all creation into existence. But when it came to you and me, He changed course. He did not just speak us into existence. He could have, but He didn't. He took existing material—the dust of the ground that He had already made—and *formed* man.

When the Bible states that God "formed" man, God chose the same Hebrew word used in other places in the Old Testament to describe a potter laboring over his clay, forming and fashioning it into a vessel of beauty. God was the Artisan meticulously molding and making us. And then He animated us by breathing into us "the breath of life." He took time, care, and effort when He created man.

THE GOSPEL

We are different from all the other created order. We are unique. Among other things, we have been given the gift of significance. We were created in the very image of God. Our significance is not found in what we accomplish or in our natural abilities. It is found way back in the very beginning when God initiated a relationship with us. Ever since then we have been on this search to recover our true significance grounded in that relationship.

We are on a search today because we abruptly lost the significance we once enjoyed. We were placed in a beautiful garden and given dominion over all of it. Talk about significance! But we lost it. Pride entered the picture. We listened to the devil's lie, bought into it, and sinfully disobeyed God.

The consequence? We were expelled from the garden (see Genesis 3). And gone was the significance we once enjoyed. Ever since then we have been on a search for our lost estate, our own significance. We have looked for it in anything and everything this world has to offer. The apostle Paul addressed this situation in the New Testament: "Through one man sin entered the world, and death through sin, and thus death spread to all men, because all sinned" (Romans 5:12). You may gain all the things that life can afford—more possessions, more power, more prestige—but your search for significance will find no end unless it ends in your restored relationship with your Creator.

God has provided a plan for us to recover the significance we once enjoyed but lost. He has made provision for us in the gift of His only Son, the Lord Jesus Christ, who came to earth to restore our lost heritage of relationship with God. Ironically, He is the One who is on a search today . . . for you. Jesus laid aside His own glory. He emptied Himself. He condescended to clothe Himself in human flesh. And He who never sinned became sin for us. He died our death . . . so we could live His life. He took our sin . . . so we could take His righteousness. If you are looking for significance, you will not find it by looking around you. King Nebuchadnezzar lifted up his eyes to heaven. Our search for significance will end when we do the same thing. By looking up to Jesus, we can reclaim what we lost.

LESSONS FROM THEN . . . FOR NOW

Across all these centuries Daniel is still teaching us how to live in a culture that, like his, has become foreign to all our truth claims and value systems. Through the pages of this volume, he has been encouraging us to never give in, give up, or give out. His three Hebrew friends have challenged us to learn to live with pressure, principle, perspective, and protection. Then King Nebuchadnezzar himself testified to each of us that the way down is up and the way up is down.

Daniel 4 leaves us with four lessons:

- *Pride*: "Those who walk in pride He is able to put down" (Daniel 4:37). Pride leads the parade of sins which God says He "hates" (Proverbs 6:16).
- *Procrastination*: "At the end of twelve months [Nebuchadnezzar] was walking about the royal palace of Babylon" (Daniel 4:29). The king reminded us of the danger of forgetting God in days of continued blessing and unheeded warnings.
- *Presumption*: "Is not this the great Babylon that I have built . . . by my mighty power and for the honor of my majesty?" (Daniel 4:30). We may presume that there will always be adequate time to do the right thing. But if we do not break from our sin, we will—like Nebuchadnezzar—be broken by it.
- *Providence*: "The Most High rules in the kingdom of men" (Daniel 4:17). God has not abdicated His

throne. He still has His own ways of showing us that He is in ultimate control.

Our contemporary culture is still waiting and watching to see if we Christians practice what we preach. If ever a culture needed to be reminded that "those who walk in pride He is able to put down," it is ours. Your search for significance will end when you come to grips with two timeless truths. First, the bad news is . . . the way down is up. But the good news is . . . the way up is down!

SECTION V

GOD AND GRAFFITI:

The Handwriting Is on the Wall

*T*hroughout recorded human history, public walls have been used as a canvas for various ideas, covering the gamut from political dissent to love messages to purely artistic endeavors. Our modern culture has enhanced and even expanded this age-old art form that we commonly call "graffiti." One has to journey all the way back to ancient Rome to find the origin of this word. It is the plural of *graffito*, which means "to scratch." It refers to drawing on a wall in such a way so it can be seen by the passing public and communicate a particular message. Graffiti was first found on the walls of the ruins of Pompeii and Rome around 50 BC. But long before the Romans coined the word, we find graffiti on the wall of a Babylonian palace one fateful night, recorded for all posterity in Daniel 5.

Across the centuries graffiti has become a worldwide phenomenon. It's a medium for communication around the world. Can we ever forget the tearing down of the Berlin Wall in 1989? It came tumbling down as we watched on our television sets. The wall was covered with graffiti on its western side. For years this fifteen-foot-high barrier separating the east and the west had expressed in graffiti the desire for a long-hoped-for freedom. During the days of the first Intifada, known as the Palestinian Uprising in Jerusalem, I personally saw the writings in green, red, and black on the walls of the Arabic sector of the Holy City, with its messages to the world of occupation and oppression. In my own city of Dallas, the city fathers have declared an underpass in the Deep Ellum district a historical landmark because of the colorful graffiti art covering its walls. Modern billboards lining our streets and highways are an extension of this ancient means of communication. Graffiti's new turf today is definitely the Internet.

But we must go back even before Pompeii and Rome, back almost five centuries earlier, to find the world's original graffiti artist in ancient Babylon. It appeared one night on a wall of the ornate banquet hall in King Belshazzar's palace.

Nebuchadnezzar was now off the scene. Twenty years had passed since his death. He had been succeeded by his son, who was subsequently assassinated by his brother-in-law who, in turn, ruled for four years until losing his life on the field of battle. He was followed by Nabonidus and his son, Belshazzar, who actually ruled briefly as co-regents. Thus, our scene now unfolds in the midst of a drunken orgy hosted by King Belshazzar.

A Message of Judgment

As the Babylonians blasphemed and partied on into the night, a strange event occurred: "The fingers of a man's hand appeared and wrote opposite the lampstand on the plaster of the wall of the king's palace; and the king saw the part of the hand that wrote" (Daniel 5:5). The writing said in bold letters, " MENE, MENE, TEKEL, UPHARSIN." (If you have ever wondered where we got our colloquialism "the handwriting is on the wall," it is right here in Belshazzar's palace.)

The finger writing on the wall that night was the very finger of God. He had a message for all the people to see, so He wrote it plainly on a large plaster wall. But what did these ancient words convey?

Enter Daniel. He was once again summoned into the presence of a king to interpret, not a dream this time, but the writing on the wall. He was no longer the handsome young Hebrew he was when he first stood before Nebuchadnezzar. He was now approaching almost ninety years of age. He looked at the wall and interpreted the graffiti:

> "This is the inscription that was written: MENE, MENE, TEKEL, UPHARSIN. This is the interpretation of each word. MENE: God has numbered your kingdom, and finished it; TEKEL: You have been weighed in the balances, and found wanting; PERES: Your kingdom has been divided, and given to the Medes and Persians." (Daniel 5:25–28)

And did it ever come true! *Mene* is an Aramaic noun from a verb meaning "to number." It means, "Your number is up. Your time has run out. You are finished. It is over." *Tekel* is a noun from the verb meaning "to weigh," as one might weigh something on a scale. Solomon reminded us that "all the ways of a man are pure in his own eyes, but the LORD weighs the spirits" (Proverbs 16:2). Belshazzar was being weighed on God's own scales that evening, and he was found wanting. Finally, *upharsin* is a noun from a verb meaning "to break into something; to separate or to divide." Not only were Belshazzar's days numbered and not only was he weighed and found wanting, but he was about to be separated from all he had ever known. The handwriting was on the wall.

A MESSAGE FOR MANY

These three words proclaim the destiny of all those people without the Lord. The words reveal the ultimate end of opportunity, the judgment that comes when we are weighed on the scales of righteousness with its demands of the law and found wanting, and the separation that follows for all eternity. Belshazzar thought he was indestructible. But now he found himself at the end of his days, weighed, found wanting, and about to be separated from all he knew and loved. These are haunting words: *Mene, Tekel, Upharsin*. The handwriting is still on the wall today. The problem is that many do not see it, so they keep partying on through life. But their days are numbered, and when weighed on the scales of God's righteousness, these people do not measure up. (None of us can.)

God, however, has not only written graffiti on Belshazzar's wall. This same finger had written before and will write again. When God sent the plagues upon ancient Egypt, Pharaoh's counselor came running to him exclaiming, "This is the finger of God!" (Exodus 8:19). When Moses was at Mount Sinai, God gave him the tablets of stone on which the Ten Commandments were written with "the finger of God" (Exodus 31:18). Centuries later, God came here to earth, clothed in human flesh, and walked among us. Once, when confronted by a woman taken in the act of adultery and the group of self-righteous Pharisees about to stone her to death, "Jesus stooped down and wrote on the ground with His finger" (John 8:6).

That fateful evening in Babylon, this same God visited Belshazzar's feast and, with His finger, wrote a message on the wall for all posterity to see and heed. The handwriting is on the wall for our contemporary culture as well. And if God doesn't judge us for our own perversion and rebellion, perhaps he should apologize to Babylon for His judgment of them. *Mene, Tekel, Upharsin* is written on our wall today. If we look closely enough, we, too, will see the finger of God. Turn the page and see how this late-night drama in a king's banquet hall played out.

16   GOD IS SPEAKING TO . . .

The fingers of a man's hand appeared and wrote opposite the lampstand on the plaster of the wall of the king's palace; and the king saw the part of the hand that wrote. Then the king's countenance changed, and his thoughts troubled him, so that the joints of his hips were loosened and his knees knocked against each other. The king cried aloud to bring in the astrologers, the Chaldeans, and the soothsayers. The king spoke, saying to the wise men of Babylon, "Whoever reads this writing, and tells me its interpretation, shall be clothed with purple and have a chain of gold around his neck; and he shall be the third ruler in the kingdom." Now all the king's wise men came, but they could not read the writing, or make known to the king its interpretation. Then King Belshazzar was greatly troubled, his countenance was changed, and his lords were astonished.

—DANIEL 5:5–9

*S*eventy years have now come and gone since we first met Daniel shortly after he was taken captive from Israel and carried into Babylon. We can study how he lived all these years and see the example he was setting to teach us today how to find our way in a culture that is losing its way. He was now no longer the young, strapping, handsome young teenager chosen by the king to be "trained in the way of the Babylonians." He was now well up into his eighties, and King Nebuchadnezzar had been off the scene for a couple of decades. But before the king died—and due to the influence of Daniel—he left us a legacy in his last words: "Now I, Nebuchadnezzar, praise and extol and honor the King of heaven, all of whose works are truth, and His ways justice. And those who walk in pride He is able to put down" (Daniel 4:37). But—like individuals—countries and cultures have a way of forgetting wisdom from the past.

Belshazzar was now on the throne. He was the grandson of Nebuchadnezzar. As Daniel 5 begins, we find that Babylon was no longer the ruling world power, although they found that hard to admit. In fact, while they were partying inside the walls, their fabulous city of Babylon was besieged by the armies of the Medes and the Persians under the able leadership of Cyrus. The greater tragedy of the Babylonian culture was that they had crumbled from within. This is the way it almost always happens to a culture that has lost its way.

OUTSIDE AND IN

Mighty Babylon was now besieged. Outside were determination and dedication; inside, denial and deterioration. Outside were preparation and planning; inside, partying and perversion. And King Belshazzar? He was feasting when he should have been fasting. Blind (figuratively) and belligerent (literally), he invited a thousand nobles of Babylon to a great party in the royal hall. This was the office party to beat all office parties—complete with wine, women, and song. All the high-dollar concubines of the kingdom were in attendance. The orgies that ensued during these godless feasts should not be described in a book such as this. Suffice it to say, they were as perverted as much of what we see in our own culture today.

As the party moved into full swing, the crowd became increasingly more intoxicated. Belshazzar sent for the golden vessels that had been brought to Babylon decades earlier from Solomon's temple in Jerusalem. For seventy years these sacred vessels, once used in the worship of the living God, had been locked away in safe storage in Babylon. But no more. In his folly, the king filled them with drink and mocked the living God by drinking from them. His drunkenness and sexual perversions didn't seem to satisfy him. He was now blaspheming the Lord God of Israel, the one true and living Lord. It was at this point, "in the same hour" (Daniel 5:5), that a man's hand began to write on the wall of the royal hall.

ENTER . . . DANIEL

At once a hush fell on the assembly. The drinking stopped. The feasting stopped. The illicit sexual acts halted. Fear rolled over the crowd in waves. "The king's countenance changed, and his thoughts troubled him, so that the joints of his hips were loosened and his knees knocked against each other" (Daniel 5:6). His face, only moments earlier flushed red by wine, now was ashen white. Fear gripped his hardened heart. His eyes were no longer squinting; they were now wide open in astonishment. His lips quivered, and his heart seemed to beat out of his chest. Yes, "it is a fearful thing to fall into the hands of the living God" (Hebrews 10:31). The handwriting was on the wall.

All eyes were on the king. He "cried aloud to bring in the astrologers, the Chaldeans, and the soothsayers. The king spoke, saying to the wise men of Babylon, 'Whoever reads this writing, and tells me its interpretation, shall be clothed with purple and have a chain of gold around his neck; and he shall be the third ruler in the kingdom'" (Daniel 5:7). Here we go again. Never learning, this king brought in the same old losers who had counseled his predecessors, but those who claim to possess the wisdom of the world are always at a loss for answers to the human heart when the handwriting is on the wall. Many in our own culture still run to those who bring no permanent help or positive hope. Now—and for good reason—King Belshazzar was "greatly troubled" (v. 9).

The queen mother appeared on the scene to remind her son that there was a man "in your kingdom in whom is the Spirit of the Holy God" (Daniel 5:11). Even today God is still on the look for men and women who will make known His truth without fear in cultures like our own. Daniel was brought into the hall. He held nothing back; he watered down nothing. He laid it out: "This is the inscription that was written: MENE, MENE, TEKEL, UPHARSIN. This is the interpretation of each word. MENE: God has numbered your kingdom, and finished it; ` TEKEL: You have been weighed in the balances, and found wanting; PERES [*PERES* is used interchangeably with *UPHARSIN*]: Your kingdom has been divided, and given to the Medes and Persians" (vv. 25–28).

NEEDED: DANIELS

This pronouncement brings us to a poignant and pertinent question: Where are the Daniels of our day speaking boldly to our corrupt culture? Where are those in whom "the Spirit of the holy God" lives and who will therefore tell it like it really is? Some people seem more interested in getting an invitation to the banquet from those in high places than speaking the truth in power even though, all the while, the handwriting is on the wall. We have raised a couple of generations in our culture who have heard little to nothing of the judgment of God and who virtually know nothing about living in the fear of the Lord.

God Himself recorded the final day of the great kingdom of Babylon, a day of judgment: "That very night Belshazzar, king of the Chaldeans, was slain. And Darius the Mede received the kingdom" (Daniel 5:30–31). Thus ended forever the once-great world power of Babylon. God was keeping His word: that very night, the "head of gold" became the "chest of . . . silver" (2:32–35). The Medes and Persians broke the Babylonian supremacy exactly as God had prophesied in His Word.

And, keeping His word, God will judge our culture and nation as well. After all, we will see in Daniel 5 several obvious parallels to our own culture. But will we heed the warning it offers, the warning that a culture like our own is doomed without a massive spiritual awakening? Simply making a few affirmations and sending some praise in God's direction—as Nebuchadnezzar did in chapters 3 and 4—will never suffice. It is time for the church to step out of its own modern Babylon, with its fading pageantry and false pride, and bring the unchanging truth into a confrontation with our culture.

How do we engage our culture? By standing tall like Daniel.

REPENT!

We have the Word of God, written with His own finger, not on a wall, but between the pages of a sacred book we call the Bible. His message to our contemporary culture has not changed: *Mene, Tekel, Upharsin.* Our own days are numbered. We, too, have been weighed on God's scale and found wanting. And eternal separation from God awaits us . . . unless we repent.

So—bottom line—what is God saying through this account of Daniel's life? Never underestimate the power of one good and godly life with character, integrity, and courage. As we are about to see, God is speaking to our Western culture about its pride, presumption, promiscuity, and perversion. The handwriting is on the wall!

17   OUR PRIDEFUL CULTURE

Daniel answered, and said before the king [Belshazzar] . . .
"But when [Nebuchadnezzar's] heart was lifted up, and his
spirit was hardened in pride, he was deposed from his kingly
throne, and they took his glory from him. Then he was driven
from the sons of men, his heart was made like the beasts, and
his dwelling was with the wild donkeys. They fed him with
grass like oxen, and his body was wet with the dew of heaven,
till he knew that the Most High God rules in the kingdom of
men, and appoints over it whomever He chooses.

But you his son, Belshazzar, have not humbled your heart,
although you knew all this. And you have lifted yourself up
against the Lord of heaven. They have brought the vessels of
His house before you, and you and your lords, your wives and
your concubines, have drunk wine from them. And you have
praised the gods of silver and gold, bronze and iron, wood and
stone, which do not see or hear or know; and the God who
holds your breath in His hand and owns all your ways, you
have not glorified."

—DANIEL 5:17, 20–23

*K*ing Belshazzar should have known better! His
problem—and it's often our own—was that he had

forgotten some valuable lessons from the past. Not the least of these was the legacy his own grandfather, King Nebuchadnezzar, had left him: "Those who walk in pride [God] is able to put down" (Daniel 4:37). And just in case anyone might be looking for a good definition of pride, Daniel now laid it out: "You have lifted yourself up against the Lord of heaven" (5:23). The phrase "lifted yourself up" means "boasted; elevated; lifted oneself up above all the rest." This is precisely what Belshazzar did this fateful night.

As the Bible teaches and as our own experiences illustrate, pride always has a way of preceding a fall. Remember that God is still in the business of putting down those who walk in pride. In fact, pride is at the very top of the list of what God hates (Proverbs 6:16–17). Ask Lucifer, once the dazzling angel of light, if those who walk in pride are not put down. Ask Adam and Eve, expelled from a beautiful paradise, if those who walk in pride are not put down. Ask King David . . . and a million other people. Ask me. Ask yourself.

Perhaps no one can testify to this truth more than Simon Peter, the rough, callus-handed fisherman who left all to follow Jesus of Nazareth. His name is synonymous with one who is brash, bold, and boastful. One time he declared to Christ, "Lord, I am ready to go with You, both to prison and to death" (Luke 22:33). Peter was prideful and confident in his own self-determination, but Jesus knew better. He looked His disciple straight in the eye: "I tell you, Peter, the rooster shall not crow this day before you will deny three times that you know Me" (v. 34). It did. And he did!

A PRECIPITOUS FALL

Ask a dozen Christians to identify for you their very favorite apostle. Without giving it a thought, the majority will say, "Simon Peter." Perhaps the reason is that he is so intensely human. We like that about him. He is like so many of us: often impulsive and even impetuous. Clearly he never expected to deny the Lord. In spite of Christ's clear and specific warning to Peter, I am convinced that a blatant denial was the furthest thing from his mind. But who of us intends to experience a spiritual downfall due to our pride? Most of us, like Simon Peter, have a blind spot regarding the degree of our pride.

Peter's denial of Jesus began with *pride*. Jesus warned him in the gentlest, most compassionate manner imaginable against letting pride rule his conversation and conduct. And Peter's response? "Lord, I am ready to go with You. It doesn't matter where. If it is prison, I'll be with You. I can handle it. Even in death, I'll be with You." It doesn't matter whether your name is Simon Peter, Nebuchadnezzar, Belshazzar . . . or your own: step one of a spiritual decline is a prideful overconfidence in the flesh. So many modern approaches to enhancing self-esteem, self-confidence, self-reliance, self-actualization, and the like are simply ways of making us feel so sure of ourselves that we move on to the dangerous ground of having confidence in the flesh.

Such pride is what gets us started on a downward path, and pride always leads to *prayerlessness*. Look at Peter in Gethsemane's garden. As Jesus was intensely praying, even to the point of sweating drops of blood, Peter was snoozing. Asleep! Right there a few feet away. Pride has a way of leading to a life that sees little need for prayer.

Now, in rapid succession, a chain reaction is set in place. Pride and prayerlessness lead to *presumption*. The next thing we see Peter do is take out his sword when the mob came to arrest Jesus. Peter took a swipe at a servant of the high priest and cut off his ear. A life of pride will lead to a life filled with all sorts of impulsive acts.

Then, in Peter's case, presumption led to a sort of *paranoia* on his part. After Christ's arrest, Peter "followed at a distance" (Luke 22:54). In fear, he now kept his distance from this Person to whom he had boasted he would never leave or forsake.

Next came *peer pressure*. Jesus was taken to the palace of Caiaphas, the high priest. Peter sat with a small crowd who had gathered in the outside courtyard around a fire. When asked if he was one of the Jesus' followers, he succumbed rapidly and readily to the peer pressure he felt. Things were going from bad to worse now as a form of *paralysis* set in. All the brash talk and words of bold allegiance—spoken just a few hours earlier—had faded from his consciousness.

Next came outright *perjury*. Open denial. Lying. "I never knew the Man!" Peter's awful downward spiral began with his pride.

Our Culture of Pride

God is speaking to us today about own prideful culture. We are really no different from Peter when it comes to our own culture's downward slide. Our nation—along with the Western culture of our grandparents and parents—once honored God openly and unashamedly. We once believed the Ten Commandments were the building block of any and every decent democracy on earth. We once acknowledged His presence in our midst in every aspect of life, whether a high school graduation, a ball game, on a city square during Christmas, or in the high places of power in our nation's capital. One leader of the free world after another openly credited God for our blessings and successes. But no more. And today the handwriting is on our own wall: *Mene, Tekel, Upharsin!*

God is weighing our hearts and speaking to us about our pride. Can you still hear His "still small voice"? (See 1 Kings 19:11–13.) If not, the handwriting is on the wall!

18   OUR PRESUMPTUOUS CULTURE

Belshazzar the king made a great feast for a thousand of his lords, and drank wine in the presence of the thousand.

—DANIEL 5:1

*B*ack to the feast. This was an invitation you didn't refuse. Or, better said, you *couldn't* refuse.

All the leaders of the kingdom, a thousand of the king's lords, gathered for what turned out to be nothing more than the Guinness Book world record for drunken orgies. And, at the same time, the armies of the Medes and the Persians were camped right outside the city walls. Talk about presumption! Here it is personified: In the king's mind, Babylon was indestructible. And yet anywhere a sentry walked around atop the fifteen-mile circumference of those great walls, the enemy was in plain view below. Belshazzar, in his pride and presumption, felt safe and secure within his walls. And, historians report, there were enough supplies in the city to last for twenty years or more.

So what did the king do? He threw a big party! His confidence was in the physical, in his seemingly impregnable, walled city. As we read these words, we are prone to ask ourselves if we are not much the same in our Western culture today. Is the same thing happening today . . . here . . . now? Is God speaking to us through the book of Daniel regarding our own presumptive culture?

WEAKENED WITHIN

It is ironic that often in those times when a man feels himself most secure in his own strength, personal peril is most imminent. The wealthy, young "fool" of whom Jesus spoke in a parable comes readily to mind at this point. The young man boasted, "I will say to my soul, 'Soul, you have many goods laid up for many years; take your ease; eat, drink and be merry'" (Luke 12:19). If you know the rest of the story, that very night the young man's soul would "be required of [him]" (v. 20). While King Cyrus besieged the city, King Belshazzar, thinking himself untouchable, threw a wild party. At the moment of his kingdom's greatest danger, his own presumption led him to party his troubles away. Or so he thought.

Belshazzar is the picture of many in our own culture who ought to know better. We have gotten away with relegating God to the closet and shutting the door on Him for so long that we think this attitude can last forever. Belshazzar was too blind to realize that the strength of a kingdom—like the strength of an individual—is never on the outside but on the inside! Babylon fell that night primarily because of presumption on the inside, not because of a power on the outside.

We are living in a culture that should be focused on the real threat from the inside instead of all those that come at us from the outside. What we see in Babylon is what we should sense in America. But we don't. Oh, every great once in a while we hear our own king say something about God much as Nebuchadnezzar had done. But we have our own way of partying on, oblivious to all the warnings around us. No longer, it seems, do our friends around the world trust us, nor do our enemies fear us as they once did. Yet many still think our own walls are impregnable. But, like Babylon, the more critical problem is that our culture is crumbling from within.

TAKE HEED!

These words of warning from the pen of the apostle Paul to the corrupt culture of Corinth are echoing down through the centuries: "Let him who thinks he stands take heed lest he fall" (1 Corinthians 10:12). We as a nation continue to presume on so many false premises.

So, yes, for those who have eyes to really see, the handwriting is on our own wall today. *Mene, Tekel, Upharsin.* Are our days numbered? Are we being weighed in the balance and found wanting? Is our own day of reckoning approaching? As He did in Babylon, God speaks those words today to our own prideful and presumptive culture.

The real strength of any kingdom—or any individual—is never on the outside. It is always on the inside! May we acknowledge that truth and the truth about our culture's demise, for the handwriting is on the wall.

While he tasted the wine, Belshazzar gave the command to bring the gold and silver vessels which his father Nebuchadnezzar had taken from the temple which had been in Jerusalem, that the king and his lords, his wives, and his concubines might drink from them.

—DANIEL 5:2

*B*abylonian culture was filled with what the Old Testament writer rather politely referred to as "concubines." This word serves to sanitize the real issue. These were kept women used for the express purposes of extramarital sexual gratification and additional procreation. Promiscuity had been woven into the very fabric of this ancient culture. And, it seems, we are no different today. We simply use more palatable terminology. Sexual permissiveness and even sexual perversions are accepted norms of the day in our Western culture. But God is not suffering from laryngitis. He has not lost His voice. He is still speaking today, and not just at the point of our pride and presumption, but also at the point of our open and blatant promiscuity.

In Daniel 5, Babylonian culture—so rich and so royal—collapsed in a moment. The people had felt secure even as they crumbled within their own hearts. Their culture made four mistakes that kept them from stopping the collapse.

- They lost all sense of *remembrance*. The present king had ignored and forgotten the lessons he could have learned from his predecessors.
- The Babylonians lost all sense of *reality*. Still thinking they were too big to fail, they wouldn't face the reality before them.
- They also lost all sense of *restraint*. Increasingly, they became a morally degenerate people. And the result?
- They lost all sense of *respect*. Nothing was sacred to them anymore.

And because history does indeed repeat itself, we should sit up on the edge of our seats and take careful note. God isn't just speaking now. He is shouting at us about our promiscuous culture.

ACUTE AMNESIA

If we are honest, we, too, have lost a sense of *remembrance*. Pride caused the king to forget the valuable lessons his grandfather had learned and left for posterity. Daniel gave pertinent insight to the problem by simply saying to Belshazzar, "You have lifted yourself up against the Lord of heaven" (Daniel 5:23). It is one thing to lift ourselves up, but quite another when we seek to replace God Himself in the process. Our culture used to honor God and credit Him unashamedly with our blessings and successes. During the days of the

First World War, President Woodrow Wilson put it thus: "A nation which does not remember what it was yesterday does not know what it is today, nor what it is trying to do. We are trying to do a futile thing if we do not know where we came from or what we have been about." Like ancient Babylon, our own culture is suffering from a form of acute amnesia.

Think back about what really made America a great nation, distinguishing us from our neighbors to the north and to the south. Canada was settled by French explorers looking for gold. Mexico was settled by Spanish explorers in search of the very same thing: gold. No matter how much effort goes into a revisionist rewriting of American history books, the truth remains that America was settled by courageous men and women who were not looking for gold, but for God. They wanted a new world in which to worship Him outside the confines and constraints of a state-controlled church.

Forever recorded in the charters of the original thirteen colonies is evidence of the absolute truth of this fact. The 1683 charter of Rhode Island reads like this: "We submit our persons, our lives and our estates to the Lordship of our Lord Jesus Christ, the King of kings and Lord of lords and to all those perfect and most absolute laws given to us in His Holy Word." Maryland's original charter reminds all her citizens that she was "formed by a pious zeal to extend the Christian gospel." Delaware's charter says it was "formed for the further propagation of the Gospel of the Lord Jesus Christ." And Connecticut? The reason for it being established was—in the words of its own charter—"to preserve the purity of the Gospel of the Lord Jesus Christ." But we have lost all sense of remembrance. How have we come so far as to allow our court systems to rule against something as simple as the placing of the Ten Commandments on a school wall? Ironically, I might add, the commandments are etched in stone over the very chairs where the Supreme Court sits. There are striking parallels to Babylonian culture and our own. First, we both have lost a sense of remembrance.

CULTURAL DECLINE

We have also lost a sense of *reality.* Outside the walls of Babylon, an enemy lurked, but inside the people couldn't have cared less. They could not bring themselves to face reality. God had given the Israelites who were in captivity three things—a Lord, a law, and a land. Three thousand years later He did the same thing for another people, for us. He gave us a Lord. (Again, for anyone who doesn't believe it, our forefathers' commitment the Lord is forever written in the charters of the original colonies and in stone in original institutions of higher learning, like Harvard and others, as well as etched in stone in multiple buildings in the nation's capital.) He gave us a law based on Israel's ancient commandments and expressed in our Constitution. And He gave us a land from which we have served as His hand extended through the decades to countries in need all over the world. The reality is that we have met the real enemy . . . and it is us.

The third mistake the Babylonians made—and we're

making—was that they had lost all sense of *restraint*. The obvious correlation between people's moral decay and their nation's decline is written in the history books of one nation after another. In his book *Our Dance Has Turned to Death*, Carl Wilson chronicled the pattern of decline in both the Greek and Roman cultures. He cited that men ceased to lead their families in spiritual and moral development. They neglected their wives and children in pursuit of material wealth and power. Marriage laws were changed in order to make divorce much easier to obtain. Because a male and a female role model were not as often in the same home, children began to develop identity problems. An increasing number of these children were abandoned, abused, aborted, molested, or undisciplined. And Wilson was not writing here about our own culture, but one that self-destructed almost two thousand years ago. History repeats itself . . . always. We, along with so many before us and so many beside us, seem to be losing our sense of remembrance, reality, and restraint.

Hearing and Obeying

Unfortunately, we are not finished yet: Babylon also lost all sense of respect. Nothing was sacred for the Babylonians anymore. Because they had now raised a couple of generations with no moral absolutes or restraints, it naturally followed that there would no longer be any respect for anything that was once held sacred. Belshazzar drank his wine from the same gold vessels that once served in the worship of Jehovah God in Solomon's temple. Before we are too quick to self-righteously condemn, we should ask our own culture—we should ask ourselves—if we have also lost a sense of remembrance, reality, restraint, and respect.

The handwriting was on the wall in Belshazzar's palace . . . and it's on ours today. It's not too late for us. God is speaking about our pride, our presumption, and our promiscuity. The real question of our time is, can we still hear His voice? And if we hear it, will we obey?

OUR PERVERTED CULTURE

While he tasted the wine, Belshazzar gave the command to bring the gold and silver vessels which his father Nebuchadnezzar had taken from the temple which had been in Jerusalem, that the king and his lords, his wives, and his concubines might drink from them. Then they brought the gold vessels that had been taken from the temple of the house of God which had been in Jerusalem; and the king and his lords, his wives, and his concubines drank from them. They drank wine, and praised the gods of gold and silver, bronze and iron, wood and stone.

—DANIEL 5:2–4

The curtain now rises on the final act of a corrupt culture. It was party time in Babylon. This was not some little wine-tasting party. The verbs indicated that Belshazzar was pouring glass after glass, goblet after goblet. He was working himself and all the others into a drunken frenzy. No restraint here. None at all.

Then Belshazzar had an idea and called for the golden vessels that had been brought from Jerusalem decades earlier and stored for safekeeping. God had called these vessels used in worship in the temple "holy." In Hebrew the word *holy* means "set apart." These goblets had been set apart for use by the priests in temple worship. But the Babylonians gave little attention to anything God had called "holy."

In the midst of all this drunken debauchery, a finger began to write those words of judgment on the wall for all to see. The drinking stopped. A hush fell over the vast room, and in walked our man Daniel. He had not been at the party, but was summoned to help interpret the handwriting. Of course no one wants a man of God around when the liquor is flowing and sexual perversions are in full swing. However, when a crisis comes, when the handwriting is on the wall, when all our worldly friends fail us miserably, how often we welcome the preacher's presence. Sooner or later the handwriting is on our own wall, and at that moment men and women don't want their drinking buddies or immoral friends. They want someone who can tell them what God is saying.

A CAPTIVE AUDIENCE

Daniel was fully aware of what was transpiring. He knew. In fact, scores of years before, the Jewish prophet Isaiah had foretold these very events (Isaiah 13:17–19). Daniel knew the Medes and the Persians were about to enter the city. After all, the handwriting was on the wall! Daniel looked around at the frightened faces. All the shouting, drinking, and sex had stopped. An eerie silence filled the hall as people seemed frozen in time. I imagine the sacred vessels were scattered on the floor and overturned on the tables. I can almost see Daniel bending down and gently picking up one of those golden goblets and gracefully, reverently, gently placing it on the table. He knew.

Daniel was the only one in the ballroom who was calm. He did what every preacher should do in a time like this: he took the word that came from God and, without fear or favor, simply revealed to them what the Almighty had said. He didn't try to make it more palatable and sugarcoat it like many in our contemporary culture do today. He just laid out God's message.

FIRST, A SERMON

Look at Daniel. Before he interpreted the writing on the wall, he preached a sermon to them. He first addressed the *origin of power*. He reminded Belshazzar that King Nebuchadnezzar's power had come from God: "The Most High God gave Nebuchadnezzar your father a kingdom and majesty, glory and honor" (Daniel 5:18). Daniel also reminded Belshazzar of the Source of all power. Belshazzar knew this . . . but he had forgotten it.

Next, Daniel pointed to the *outcome of pride*. He continued with his account of Nebuchadnezzar: "When his heart was lifted up, and his spirit was hardened in pride, he was deposed from his kingly throne, and they took his glory from him" (Daniel 5:20). He reminded everyone that the kingdom was lost because of—in one word—pride! Daniel had reminded them all that "the Most High rules in the kingdom of men" (4:32).

Then, looking straight into King Belshazzar's eyes,

Daniel said, "You . . . have not humbled your heart, although you knew all this [about Nebuchadnezzar's pride and how God dealt with him]" (Daniel 5:22). Yes, the king "knew all of this"! And yet he continued in pride and did nothing about it. The irony of the whole episode is that while we, too, know better, many of us party on in our culture when the handwriting is on our own wall.

NEXT, THE INTERPRETATION

Mene, Tekel, Upharsin. Daniel then dug into the lexical roots of those words of warning on the wall: the Babylonians' days were numbered. They were weighed on God's scales and found wanting. They were about to be separated forever. The opportunity had passed. Judgment was no longer *coming*; it was literally at the door. It had arrived that very night.

Mene warned, "Your days are numbered." This Aramaic word means time has finally run out. It is finished. It is over. No more opportunities to do the right thing. No more second chances. And that is the way it happens: suddenly. Often when we least expect it, the finger of God writes on the wall. This is one of God's truths that, unfortunately, is seldom ever heard from our culturally and politically correct pulpits today: "It is appointed for men to die once, but after this the judgment" (Hebrews 9:27). The Bible challenges us "to number our days" (Psalm 90:12). We are allotted just so many days. They are already numbered. There is coming a day when God will write on our own wall *Mene.*

With *Tekel* God was painting the picture of a scale with

His standard on one side and ours on the other. But we don't measure up. God's standard is the law—and who could ever measure up to the righteous demands of His law? Not me. Not you. So, moved and motivated by His love for us, God sent His only Son, the Lord Jesus, to take our place on the scales of life. Jesus met the righteous standard required. He never sinned. He was not found wanting in any way. And so, on a Roman cross, He took our sin that we might be free from the righteous demands of the law and be able to find favor with God through Him.

Then came the final fateful word: *Upharsin*. Note the scene in Belshazzar's ballroom. In the midst of this utter terror and fear stood one figure in perfect peace. There was not a hint of fear in his face nor terror in his eyes. There was no guilt in his heart. He knew the One who wrote the words on the wall. Judgment holds no fear for those, like Daniel, who know the living Lord.

Now, the Judgment

"That very night Belshazzar, king of the Chaldeans was slain. And Darius the Mede received the kingdom, being about sixty-two years old" (Daniel 5:30–31).

While the Babylonians partied, the Medes and the Persians had been busy at work diverting the Euphrates River that flowed under the walls of the city. What once was a mighty river had become nothing more than a riverbed. Instead of trying to scale over the walls or dig through them—both of which were utter impossibilities—the enemy simply walked on a dry riverbed under the walls and into the city. God's judgment is sure and certain. There is not a wall high enough nor thick enough to prevent a man (or a nation) from falling when God writes these words on the wall: *Mene. Tekel. Upharsin.*

Who of us really knows how close our own culture is to *mene*? Who of us knows how close we may be ourselves to seeing the finger of God write out the word *tekel*? Or worse, *upharsin*?

There is, after all, a last night for every nation and for every individual when the handwriting is on the wall. Daniel's words of warning to the king should be heard by every one of us: it is God who "holds your breath in His hand and owns all your ways" (Daniel 5:23). Do you really believe that? Take a deep breath. Right now. Go ahead. Every single breath you breathe is a gift from God. He "holds your breath in His hand" right now. And He owns and knows "all your ways." Yes, "the Most High rules in the kingdom of men."

As we watch and witness the end of this once mighty culture of Babylon, we cannot help but draw some parallels with our own. We often think that we, too, are impregnable, indestructible. Babylon fell because of pride: they feasted when they should have fasted. They fell because of presumption: they presumed they could get away with anything. Promiscuity played a pathetic part in their downfall: they chose unrestrained revelry while destruction was at the door. And their culture had become so perverted that the end came with a feeble and fatal mockery of God.

As we seek to find our way in a culture that has lost its way, we have much to learn from this code left us by Daniel. It is not too late. But God still has His own ways of using graffiti, and one day the handwriting will be on the wall for each of us. Yes, the Most High still rules in the affairs of men. He always has . . . and He always will!

SECTION VI

INTEGRITY

Don't Leave Home Without It

*I*t seems with each passing day we are sinking a little deeper into the quicksand of cultural collapse. For those of us who, like Daniel, seek to live *in* the world but not *of* the world, what is the single most important attribute we need as we strive to influence the culture in a positive and productive way?

Some people quickly point to *intellect*. After all, they argue, knowledge is power in our world. The greater our intellectual edge over others, the better we can gain the upper hand. Others quickly say that it isn't intellect as much as it is *intensity*, that passion accompanied by a spirit of conquest becomes contagious. Still others argue it is *insight*, that is, good old common sense, the ability to see wisely into the issues, and discernment for addressing them. However, in the final analysis, the single most important attribute of those who make a lasting difference for good in a collapsing culture like our own is . . . *integrity*!

We have all known men and women who possessed tremendous intellect and persuasive abilities to influence many, but who ended up having little to no integrity and have since been forgotten. We can also remember those who possessed an inordinate amount of intensity and passion for their task. However, they had little to no integrity, so they, too, offered the culture little, if any, positive influence. We have also come into contact with those who possessed keen insight and the ability to make wise decisions, but who ultimately revealed they had no integrity. They lost their voice as well. If we are going to find our way in a culture that has lost its way, we must be people of lasting integrity.

INTEGRITY ILLUSTRATED

Daniel certainly had a high level of intellect. We read that he was "gifted in all wisdom, possessing knowledge" (Daniel 1:4). And talk about intensity for the task! He was the epitome of passion. He "purposed in his heart that he would not defile himself" (v. 8). As for insight, not only was he gifted in wisdom and knowledge; he was "quick to understand" (v. 4). He keenly discerned the meaning of Nebuchadnezzar's dream and described in detail the message of the handwriting on the wall of Belshazzar's palace. However, it was Daniel's personal integrity that truly set him apart from all others in the kingdom and enabled him to achieve such incredible success. The Bible says, "Daniel distinguished himself above the governors and satraps, because an excellent spirit was in him" (6:3). Daniel is exhibit A of the fact that those who influence others and engage their culture for good are men and women of impeccable integrity.

Integrity can be defined as "the steadfast and constant adherence to a moral or an ethical code." It is "the state or quality that strives to be complete, free of the corrupting influences of improper motives or methods." The thesaurus pairs *integrity* with such words as *honesty, completeness*, and *incorruptibility*. In the language of the New Testament, the word *integrity* translates a complex Greek word containing a negative prefix, the preposition *through*, and the noun *corruption*. The word very literally describes a man or a woman in whom runs "no corruption through them." *Integrity* suggests a consistency between what we do in public and who we are in private. That is to say, what you see in public of a person of integrity is what he or she is in private.

Integrity is what causes the professional golfer to report his disqualifying infraction when no one else even noticed it. It is what motivates a witness to tell the whole truth from the witness stand when no one else would know if she were less than truthful. It is personal integrity that keeps men and women in the workforce from cheating on overtime hours and expense accounts. And it is our personal integrity that serves to keep us honest when April 15 rolls around each year and the IRS comes looking for our money. Integrity is what keeps us faithful to our spouses when we are away from home on a business trip.

Our contemporary culture is desperately in need of men and women of integrity. Too many of our national leaders, on both sides of the political aisle, have failed miserably on this point. With increasing regularity, another gate swings open to reveal high-profile individuals living with little or no integrity. Our culture has gone from Watergate to Irangate to Monicagate and on and on. Our corrupt culture is the product of leaders in high places who are still debating what "the meaning of *is* is." No wonder our young people question if character really counts anymore.

Our culture is crippled by a lack of integrity at every level of society. Too many local municipalities, like my own, have been dragged through the mire of widespread corruption and investigations of wrongdoing in their city governments and school systems. It is not uncommon to hear of those who resign from public office in disgrace before they are publicly exposed or indicted for some form of corruption. Sadly, there are religious leaders who score no better on the report card of personal integrity. Even as I type these very words, I heard just today of another high-profile pastor who has resigned due to a lack of personal integrity.

CHARACTER COUNTS

What does all this have to do with the familiar story of Daniel in the lions' den that we now approach in Daniel 6? If, as a child, we ever heard Bible stories, the story of Daniel in the lions' den was more than likely near the top of the list. Pictures of Daniel lying down with the docile lions adorn the walls of many nurseries. For most, the focus of the story is Daniel's miraculous deliverance. But the real message has to do with Daniel's conduct not while he was in the lions' den but before he ever got there! It is a message about integrity: character does count, and God Himself honors integrity.

Throughout these pages we have watched Daniel, time and again, impact the culture around him. He could have lived with resentment and joined the other exiles in hanging their harps on the willows and losing their song. But he rested in the fact that God was in control, that God Himself held the remote control in His own hand. Daniel knew that God also kept His finger on the thermostat when his three friends ended up in the fiery furnace. Daniel influenced a pagan culture primarily because he lived a life of integrity.

You might have the highest intellect in the room, you might be moved and motivated by an intensity manifesting itself in contagious passion, you might have keen insight to cut through to the heart of the issues of life, but if you don't live with integrity, you will join the many others on the ash heap of what might have been.

Character does count, and those who influence their culture have one thing in common: like Daniel, they are men and women of integrity. Integrity is your most valuable attribute. Don't leave home without it.

21   We All Live in Four Different Worlds

So the governors and satraps sought to find some charge against Daniel concerning the kingdom; but they could find no charge or fault, because he was faithful; nor was there any error or fault found in him.

—DANIEL 6:4

*W*e will begin finding our way through a culture that has lost its way when we begin to realize that each of us lives simultaneously in four very distinct spheres of life and therefore influence.

You live in a *private world*. There is a part of your existence that no one else ever enters. Not even those closest to you—not your husband or wife or best friend—live in your private world and know your secret and private thoughts. No one goes there. No one enters your private world except you—and the God who placed in you DNA like no one else's on the planet. He is the only One who searches your heart and knows all your private thoughts.

You also live in a *personal world*. You share this sphere of life with only a small circle of intimate family members and perhaps a few friends who truly know you well. This is a small world. It only consists of the very few people who know who you really are behind closed doors.

These concentric circles of life widen: you also live in a *professional world*. This broader world contains scores, perhaps hundreds, of people who know you in a professional setting. You interact in this world every day at the office, on the job, at school, and in the social and civic arena.

Finally, you live in a *public world*, the widest sphere of influence where people form opinions of you for good or for bad. In this world are people who may not know you professionally, much less personally, and for certain not privately. Yet when they hear your name mentioned, they have an opinion about you. Some often refer to the person you are in this world as your public persona.

Keep these four worlds in mind as we consider why so many people in our modern culture live with so little integrity.

Integrity's Roots

A lot of us are confused as to which world is most important for engaging our culture as Daniel did his so successfully. We have all witnessed individuals who seek to mask their lack of integrity by attempting to portray a positive public image. They hire public relations gurus and touch up their photos in an attempt to be seen as something they truly might not be. However, in the professional world with its daily dealings, a lack of integrity becomes a bit more difficult to disguise.

Then, once we get home in the evening and shut the door, it is virtually impossible to keep up the act around those who know us best. Many parents have lost their kids to the culture because they saw their mom or dad be one way in the public and professional world, but someone quite different in the personal arena of life. Then, in our private world, alone with God Himself, the jig is up: there is absolutely no hiding anything from Him.

This brings us to an important intersection and a defining question: Where is integrity rooted? Some seem to think it is rooted in the public world, so they are busy spinning their image into the personal personas they want people to see. But integrity is not rooted in the public life. Its presence—or its absence—is only revealed there. Ultimately, our behavior in our public world will reveal for all to see whether we are men and women of integrity.

Some argue that integrity is rooted in the professional setting, and it seems to make sense. After all, this is where we deal with others in business. Thus, some say, it is here in the professional world where integrity takes root. Our integrity, however, is not rooted in the professional world, but it can be reinforced there by our determined and disciplined efforts to deal honorably with people in our professional settings.

Then—and we are getting closer to integrity's roots—there are those who say integrity is rooted in the intensely close relational dynamics of our personal world, where we're alone with those who know us best. This possibility seems logical, but integrity is not rooted in the personal world. It is simply reflected in our relationships with those who know us best. If you want to know if I have integrity, you should ask my wife or my kids. They are the ones who know me better than anyone else in the world.

So, by the process of elimination and the principles of logic, we find that integrity is rooted in the private world, that part of us that is alone with God, that part of us that will live as long as God lives, which is forever. And when integrity has established its deep, strong roots in our private world, it will be reflected in our personal world. Our own family and our closest friends will see reflected in our personal relationships the integrity that flows from our deeper private life. Then, as our influence widens to our professional world, our honest dealings with others—what we say and how we act—will reinforce the standard of integrity we choose to live by. Ultimately, our integrity will be revealed for God's own glory in our public world.

To summarize, integrity is conceived in the private world, birthed in the personal world, grows in the professional world, and matures in the public world. We are about to see how these four worlds formed the foundation of Daniel's interests and influence and enabled him to make a huge impact on his pagan culture.

22 INTEGRITY IS ROOTED IN OUR PRIVATE LIVES

It pleased Darius to set over the kingdom one hundred and twenty satraps, to be over the whole kingdom; and over these, three governors, of whom Daniel was one, that the satraps might give account to them, so that the king would suffer no loss. Then this Daniel distinguished himself above the governors and satraps, because an excellent spirit was in him; and the king gave thought to setting him over the whole realm.

—DANIEL 6:1–3

After the fall of Babylon, the nation went through a complete overhaul. Now, under the control of Darius the Mede, it was reorganized into one hundred and twenty districts with a satrap (governor) over each one: a satrap was delegated authority over all local matters. Over these satraps were three governors who were assigned to administer the affairs of the kingdom. Daniel was elevated into a leadership position and virtually put in charge of the entire kingdom: "The king gave thought to setting him over the whole realm" (Daniel 6:3). Not bad for a boy who started out as a captive and was plopped into a new world with a different language and an entirely different culture.

What was it about Daniel that caused him to stand out above all his peers at every stage of his life? Time and again we find him rising to the surface above all others. Something was different about him. When you put it all under the microscope and focus in clearly, it is obvious that it was his character and his integrity that he kept rooted daily in his own private world. The Bible put its finger squarely on it: "An excellent spirit was in him" (Daniel 6:3). It was not because of all his unique gifts and accomplishments evident from the outside, but because of what was inside him. We call it *integrity*. An excellent spirit was within Daniel. And "within" is where our integrity is rooted: in our private world alone with God.

Two Men of Integrity

Daniel excelled and was promoted because of an inner strength. In our fast-paced, VIP world of self-promotion, with its "who you know" mentality, integrity in the private life is becoming a lost quality. We see those who are elevated to places and positions of promise because of who they know or how many backs they have slapped while climbing the ladder to success. But the people who make a lasting difference in their cultures are those men and women who ascend because of what is on the inside. Daniel was elevated in the new kingdom, not because of his powerful connections or his political correctness, but because he was a man of integrity.

It was integrity—not intelligence or intensity or insight—that got him to this position of incredible authority and responsibility. Integrity comes from within. It is not rooted in the public life, nor the professional life, nor even the personal life. Integrity finds its root system in our private world, in the secret place where Christ-life replaces self-life.

At this writing, Billy Graham is approaching the century mark of life and in his declining years. By the time some are reading these words, he will have gone home to his heavenly reward.

It was my personal joy to be called his pastor during my years of service at the First Baptist Church in Dallas, where he kept his church membership for decades. What was it about this man that caused him to be influential and trusted by so many people across several decades? Scores of times in interviews with the print media and on television talk shows he was asked, "Why you? Why have you had such a worldwide platform? Why have kings and presidents consistently sought your counsel?"

For those of us who have known Dr. Graham, the answer is obvious. It is not because of what he has been in public, and he has spoken to multiplied millions all over the world. Dr. Graham has been influential because of what he has been in private that continues to impact his public persona. Personal integrity is the single factor that has consistently separated him from others. Over the years there have been others with keener minds and more persuasive speech. But long ago they fell out of the race. Integrity is what elevated

Billy Graham to a position of influence. Integrity rooted in his private world alone with God. King Solomon had it right when he said, "The integrity of the upright guides them" (Proverbs 11:3 esv).

The exiled Daniel, living in the pagan culture of Babylon, was another person of impeccable integrity who possessed "an excellent spirit" (Daniel 6:3). Daniel rooted his life in his private world, and the Spirit of the living God led him in life. What is inside of you brings out integrity, not what is outside of you. Integrity comes with the inner choice to live by God's principles, not by outer promotion.

Spirit, Soul, Body

This is a good time for each of us to ask ourselves how we think about ourselves. Would you use the word *excellent* to describe your own spirit? Do you think of yourself as a body who just happens to have a spirit-soul within? Many today are primarily body conscious; we spend most of our time consumed with our bodies. We tan them, we tone them, and some of us even tuck them. But the body is simply the house we are residing in as we journey through this world. The body is nothing more . . . and nothing less. The real you is your spirit, that part of you that is alive within your body and will still be alive long after your body has gone back to the dust from which it came.

Integrity is rooted in our private world. So if we remain primarily body conscious, then self-exaltation and self-promotion easily raise their ugly heads in our relationships.

Pride exhibited in the personal arena spills over into the professional world and, ultimately, flows into the public arena. However, when we begin to think of ourselves as spirit beings, when we become more spirit conscious than we are body conscious, we will start rooting our integrity where it really grows: in our private world alone with God. We all are simply spirit-soul beings who happen to be living in bodies that are deteriorating with each passing day and will eventually die and be buried in the ground. True integrity must therefore be rooted in our spirit, that part of us that is immaterial and the part of us that will live forever.

STRUCTURAL INTEGRITY

Like many cities in America, my city of Dallas is seeing an incredible resurrection in its downtown community. One new skyscraper after another is being erected in the new city center. It is common to hear architects, engineers, or builders say, "That building has structural integrity." What exactly do they mean by that phrase? These experts are saying that the tall, majestic skyscraper reaching up to the heavens stands steady only because of the unseen foundation that is dug deep into the earth and that the building's infrastructure of the steel beams is solidly constructed. It is this hidden life of a building that gives it structural integrity. And so it is with us: our own integrity must be rooted in our private life, there in the secret place hidden from the view of others. Like everyone who has gone before us, we, too, will stand or fall on our own structural integrity.

Jesus concluded His Sermon on the Mount with a story that illustrates this very truth. It is the story of the wise man who built his home on the foundation of solid rock. Jesus was speaking of a man of integrity. When a listener asked about the meaning of this message, in point-blank fashion Jesus replied that the wise builder was a man who heard the Word of God and put it into practice in his daily life (Matthew 7:24–25). Personal integrity, rooted in our private life, is protected and strengthened by our time alone in the secret place of our private world with our heavenly Father.

Integrity Is Reflected in Our Personal Lives

So the governors and satraps sought to find some charge against Daniel concerning the kingdom; but they could find no charge or fault, because he was faithful; nor was there any error or fault found in him. Then these men said, "We shall not find any charge against this Daniel unless we find it against him concerning the law of his God."

—DANIEL 6:4–5

*W*hen we root our integrity in the secret place of our private world, it will soon be reflected in our personal world as we relate to those who know us best and love us most. Our transparency and integrity will be reflected in our countenance and conduct as we interact and talk with the family members and close friends who inhabit our personal lives. Those people with whom we share life's most memorable moments will readily observe our faithfulness to God's standards of honesty and uprightness. Even when the winds of personal pressures, public opinion, and political expediency blow against us, our integrity will be reflected in our personal dealings with those closest to us.

We now see the results of Daniel rooting his own integrity in the private place. It is reflected in his personal life with those closest to him. He held close to an inner circle of friends, not the least of whom were Shadrach, Meshach, and Abed-Nego. As we journey through this biblical book that bears his name, time and time again we find Daniel's integrity being reflected in his personal relationships.

Daniel lived a life of purity and transparency in the professional world (which we'll look at more in the next chapter): "He was faithful; nor was there any error or fault found in him" (Daniel 6:4). This is quite a statement about someone! Think about it—and about who said it. Those officials who sat in endless meetings with him, worked on projects with him, critiqued and were critiqued by him, dined a thousand times with him, and observed him day in and day out said, "He was faithful." Daniel's word was his bond, and he could always be depended on to do the right thing. Daniel knew it was never right to do wrong and never wrong to do right. He never changed with the shifting winds of public opinion or personal pressures. His integrity, rooted in his private life, was reflected in his personal as well as his professional life.

A POINT OF VULNERABILITY

An interesting observation can be noted here in Daniel 6: people who are always in competition with others, who are self-promoters protecting their own turf, become quite uncomfortable when someone with integrity comes on the scene. They become afraid they will be exposed in contrast.

Note the plot developing in Daniel 6 as a group of devious individuals staked out Daniel's house like investigative reporters hiding in the bushes with hidden cameras. They bugged his room. They tried everything to catch him doing something wrong. But Daniel's life was beyond reproach. He avoided even the appearance of evil. So the Bible records, "They could find no charge or fault, because he was faithful" (v. 4).

These jealous men investigating Daniel and hoping to find something on him that could sabotage his place of ascended leadership could find nothing. So these evildoers devised a plot to entrap him. They decided they would "not find any charge against this Daniel unless we find it against him concerning the law of his God" (Daniel 6:5). So they went to King Darius with a proposal directed at his ego. "Let's make a new decree," they said. This was their suggestion: "Whoever petitions any god or man for thirty days, except you, O king, shall be cast into the den of lions" (v. 7). They went on to say that they had consulted with all the governors of the kingdom and there was unanimous support for establishing this royal statute. But that was a blatant lie. All had *not* been consulted: Daniel knew nothing of this.

The plan for getting Daniel off the scene and out of the way was foolproof. They appealed to the king's ego and encouraged him to make this decree "according to the law of the Medes and the Persians" (Daniel 6:8). This simply meant that the new law was irrevocable and could never be broken. It was their way of putting man in the place of God—and our own culture is pretty good at this today. This was not just a Medeo-Persian sin but is the sin of our own day as well.

The Plan Unfolds

These plotters were convinced of three things. One, King Darius would not—in fact *could* not—reverse the decree once it was in place. Two, Daniel would never think of denying his faith in God. And, three, their plan was foolproof. All that was left to do was put it in place.

Darius issued the decree. All eyes were now on Daniel. What would he do? How would he respond to the end of his religious liberty? "Now when Daniel knew that the writing was signed, he went home. And in his upper room, with his windows opened toward Jerusalem, he knelt down on his knees three times that day, and prayed and gave thanks before his God, as was his custom since early days" (Daniel 6:10). Daniel's integrity, long rooted in the private world, was now reflected in his personal world. Daniel kept his prayer schedule. Consistency was his theme.

All Daniel had to do to save his skin was to stop praying openly for a month. He could have shut the windows so no one could see. Or he could have talked to God in the darkness of the night as he lay on his bed. He could have reasoned within himself that God surely knew his heart as well as the circumstances. But Daniel was consistent, and that is a mark of a man of integrity. What showed up in his personal life was what he was in his private life.

Look at Daniel. He knelt at his set time and prayed. And

his prayer was one of thanksgiving. He thanked God in days of delight when everything seemed to go his way, and now he thanked God in days of distress when all seemed to be going against him. Daniel did not wait until the crisis hour to pray. Having regular times of prayer was "his custom." This consistency had been the constant practice of his personal life since his teen years, when he first purposed in his heart not to eat the king's meat (Daniel 1:8). Clearly Daniel was a man of integrity.

BEING LIKE DANIEL

Like Daniel, we are living in times of tremendous cultural change. Consider a few examples.

First, the byword of our modern Western world is *tolerance*. This word once meant that we respected other people's beliefs and truth claims without necessarily accepting them. But today *tolerance* has a new definition in our culture. It has been redefined to mean that all truth claims are valid and should be accepted as such. When one believes all truth claims are valid, there is no longer room for moral absolutes. Relativism is on the march today, waving high its flag of tolerance.

Second, the truth of our day is that we have what we tolerate, as we have already seen earlier in Daniel. And we not only have today what we tolerated yesterday; we will have tomorrow what we tolerate today.

Third, finding our way in the midst of a culture that has lost its way demands personal integrity. Daniel showed us that to make a difference in our world, with its crumbling culture, our personal integrity is a must.

You may be the brightest bulb in the room when it comes to intellect or the most passionate person around when it comes to intensity, but without integrity you will never be a person of influence. Daniel rooted his integrity in his private world—in his relationship with God—and his integrity was reflected in his personal and professional worlds: "He was faithful; nor was there any error or fault found in him" (Daniel 6:4). God grant that the same be said of you . . . and me.

24   INTEGRITY IS REINFORCED IN OUR PROFESSIONAL LIVES

So the governors and satraps sought to find some charge against Daniel concerning the kingdom; but they could find no charge or fault, because he was faithful; nor was there any error or fault found in him. Then these men said, "We shall not find any charge against this Daniel unless we find it against him concerning the law of his God."

So these governors and satraps thronged before the king, and said thus to him: "King Darius, live forever! All the governors of the kingdom, the administrators and satraps, the counselors and advisors, have consulted together to establish a royal statute and to make a firm decree, that whoever petitions any god or man for thirty days, except you, O king, shall be cast into the den of lions. Now, O king, establish the decree and sign the writing, so that it cannot be changed, according to the law of the Medes and Persians, which does not alter." Therefore King Darius signed the written decree.

Now when Daniel knew that the writing was signed, he went home. And in his upper room, with his windows open toward Jerusalem, he knelt down on his knees three times that day, and prayed and gave thanks before his God, as was his custom since early days.

—DANIEL 6:4–10

*I*f our integrity is rooted in our private life and reflected in our personal life, it will be reinforced in our professional life, in our daily dealings with those in the business world. It is of note to observe that when Daniel's jealous peers sought to find fault with him, they sought to find it "concerning the kingdom" (Daniel 6:4). That is, they looked closely at the government affairs of Daniel's professional life. Those who have integrity find that it is reinforced at the office or on the job. One of the first places integrity—or the lack thereof—shows up is in our place of employment.

The men jealous of Daniel's job searched and searched but could find no flaws in Daniel's discharge of his assigned duties. He was the epitome of what King Solomon had described: "The righteous man walks in his integrity" (Proverbs 20:7). Integrity is always reinforced as it is beaten out on the anvil of personal experience in the marketplace. Business owners are quick to say that one of their biggest challenges is finding dependable and dedicated personnel. Many are not nearly as concerned about outsiders stealing from them as they are insiders. Kickbacks are commonplace in many businesses. Integrity is a lost trait in the professional life of many people. But integrity remains the best path for engaging and influencing a culture, especially in our day-to-day dealings with those in the professional setting.

INTEGRITY IN THE WORKPLACE

If you are a person of integrity, it will surface and stand out in the workplace. The apostle Paul made this crystal clear in his cyclical letter to the Ephesians when he offered this guideline for the workplace: "Be obedient to those who are your masters . . . in sincerity of heart, as to Christ" (6:5). Men and women of integrity are recognized in the marketplace because of the way they carry out their assigned tasks. These followers of Christ recognize His authority not only over every aspect of their lives but also in sports, on the freeway, in the community, at school, and in government. Why shouldn't we also recognize and respect authority in our professional settings?

In our professional lives, when we show up for work on time and we perform our duties with excellence, we are doing what integrity demands and reinforcing what has been rooted in us. People of integrity realize that their time on the job is not their own; it belongs to their employer. We have no right to use this time for our own personal endeavors when we are being compensated to use it in our employer's best interest. If we arrive late for work, take a little extra time for lunch, extend a few breaks, or handle personal affairs on our computer, we are as guilty of stealing as the one who takes money from the petty cash drawer for personal use.

People who influence the culture around them are people of integrity who faithfully perform their duties in their professional world. In the workplace we are to work "not with eyeservice, as men-pleasers, but as bondservants of Christ, doing the will of God from the heart" (Ephesians 6:6). Paul agreed that integrity rooted in the private life—that is, "from the heart"—will not only be reflected in our personal dealings but will be reinforced in our professional ones as well.

"As to the Lord"

It is in the marketplace, not the church, where we can have the greatest impact on our culture and begin to transform it through our examples of personal integrity. We are not to be "men-pleasers," as Paul called them. Those who desire to influence our own culture are not governed by popular views or public opinion polls. Why? Because our integrity emanates "from the heart" and is reinforced in the professional setting.

Paul concluded his discourse on personal integrity in the marketplace by stating that we are to reinforce our integrity by doing our work "with goodwill doing service, as to the Lord, and not to men" (Ephesians 6:7). People with integrity work with a conscious awareness that they are serving the Lord whether they are standing all day on an assembly line, working in a textile mill, sitting behind a computer in a glass office building, caring for people in a hospital, loving on kids in a day care, teaching in a classroom, or making decisions behind a big mahogany desk on the top floor. Men and women of integrity are honest and honorable whatever their workplace. Furthermore, working "as to the Lord, not to men" gives our labor and our effort a new dignity. When a waiter serves "as to the Lord," he will do so with a dignity that has a positive effect on the ones served. When a medical doctor attends to a sick patient "as to the Lord," she will do so with respect for the individual.

Our culture is increasingly resembling the culture Daniel found in exile. Think about who engaged and actually transformed that culture. It was not the preachers and religious leaders who came from Jerusalem in the exile. It was the laymen. Men like Daniel and later Nehemiah, civil servants and even politicians, faithful laymen who reinforced their integrity in their professional life, and the world stood up and took notice. Daniel was a man of integrity and, because of this, he stood out above the others in the marketplace of ideas.

Again, the best place to engage and influence our crumbling culture is in our professional world. Integrity is never rooted in the marketplace: people don't often begin a life of integrity when they arrive in the work world. We must be living with integrity before we enter the business world. Keeping our integrity rooted deep in our own private life is essential if we expect to reinforce it in the professional world. If we ever expect to make a difference in the culture, we cannot leave our integrity at home when we go to work.

INTEGRITY IS REVEALED IN OUR PUBLIC LIVES

Then these men assembled and found Daniel praying and making supplication before his God. And they went before the king, and spoke concerning the king's decree: "Have you not signed a decree that every man who petitions any god or man within thirty days, except you, O king, shall be cast into the den of lions?"

The king answered and said, "The thing is true, according to the law of the Medes and Persians, which does not alter."

So they answered and said before the king, "That Daniel, who is one of the captives from Judah, does not show due regard for you, O king, or for the decree that you have signed, but makes his petition three times a day."

And the king, when he heard these words, was greatly displeased with himself, and set his heart on Daniel to deliver him; and he labored till the going down of the sun to deliver him. Then these men approached the king, and said to the king, "Know, O king, that it is the law of the Medes and Persians that no decree or statute which the king establishes may be changed."

So the king gave the command, and they brought Daniel and cast him into the den of lions. But the king spoke, saying to Daniel, "Your God, whom you serve continually, He will deliver you." Then a stone was brought and laid on the mouth of the den, and the king sealed it with his own signet ring and with the signets of his lords, that the purpose concerning Daniel might not be changed.

Now the king went to his palace and spent the night fasting; and no musicians were brought before him. Also his sleep went from him. Then the king arose very early in the morning and went in haste to the den of lions. And when he came to the den, he cried out with a lamenting voice to Daniel. The king spoke, saying to Daniel, "Daniel, servant of the living God, has your God, whom you serve continually, been able to deliver you from the lions?"

Then Daniel said to the king, "O king, live forever! My God sent His angel and shut the lions' mouths, so that they have not hurt me, because I was found innocent before Him; and also, O king, I have done no wrong before you." Now the king was exceedingly glad for him, and commanded that they should take Daniel up out of the den. So Daniel was taken up out of the den, and no injury whatever was found on him, because he believed in his God.

And the king gave the command, and they brought those men who had accused Daniel, and they cast them into the den of lions—them, their children, and their wives; and the lions overpowered them, and broke all their bones in pieces before they ever came to the bottom of the den.

—DANIEL 6:11–24

ike the professional world, the public arena is not an easy place to start from scratch in an effort to become a person of integrity. One reason is that, in our culture, like Daniel's, it is not always true that when we do wrong we will be punished and when we do right we will be rewarded. At times the reverse seems true, challenging our commitment to do what is right. We are about to see how doing right was not rewarded in the case of our friend Daniel. Just when the situation looked hopeless, though, Daniel was delivered from death "because he believed in his God" (Daniel 6:23). What he was in the private, secret place—a committed follower of God—was ultimately revealed in the public square.

This was quite a night recorded here for all posterity in Daniel 6 as Daniel found himself the companion of a bunch of hungry lions. He had been thrown into their den, but he slept like a baby right in their midst.

And King Darius was amazed and relieved. Duped by Daniel's enemies to sign the decree that mandated what appeared to be Daniel's death, Darius stayed up all night, pacing back and forth in confusion and concern. At dawn he rushed to the lions' den, cupped his hands around his mouth, and shouted, "Daniel, servant of the living God, has your God, whom you serve continually, been able to deliver you from the lions?" (Daniel 6:20). Daniel stirred, rubbed his eyes, stretched out his arms, yawned, wiped the lion hair from his head where he had pillowed it, and answered, "O king, live forever! My God sent His angel and shut the lions'

mouths, so they have not hurt me, because I was found innocent before Him; and also, O king, I have done no wrong
before you" (vv. 21–22). The king's question is the question
our culture is asking today: Is our God whom we serve able
to deliver us?

A Public Testimony

Daniel had kept his faith in God, a mark of true integrity that
is rooted deep in one's private world. It always follows that
integrity is ultimately revealed in the public world for God's
glory and our good. There is a lesson here for us. Daniel was
in the lions' den not because he had done wrong but because
he had done right. We all know of people who, like Daniel,
have paid a great price for actually doing what was right.
But, when all is said and finally done, God—who will never
abdicate His throne—will right all wrongs. What we see in
Daniel's experience is that, in the final analysis, our integrity will be revealed in the public world as a testimony to our
faith and our God.

Upon being delivered from the lions' den, Daniel's
integrity was on public display. He took no credit for his
deliverance. He was quick to say, "My God sent His angel
and shut the lions' mouths" (Daniel 6:22). People of integrity
do not take personal credit for something they did not do.

In response, Darius made this startling decree:

*To all peoples, nations, and languages that dwell in all the
earth:*

> *Peace be multiplied to you.*
> *I make a decree that in every dominion of my*
> > *kingdom men must tremble and fear before the*
> > *God of Daniel.*
> > *For He is the living God,*
> > *And steadfast forever;*
> > *His kingdom is the one which shall not be*
> > > *destroyed,*
> > *And His dominion shall endure to the end.*
> > *He delivers and rescues,*
> > *And He works signs and wonders*
> *In heaven and on earth,*
> > *Who has delivered Daniel from the power of the*
> *lions. (Daniel 6:25–27)*

Even a lost culture will stop and take notice of a person of integrity when that integrity is, sooner or later, revealed in the public world.

Private, Personal, Professional, and Public Integrity

So what do we really learn from Daniel's experience in the midst of the lions?

We learn that our integrity must be rooted in our private life. Prayer should be our number one priority. In Daniel's own value system, his private time alone with his God was his highest priority.

We learn that integrity is reflected in our personal lives. How we respond and react in our personal relationships with those who know us best is directly correlated to the strength of our own private life with the Lord.

We also learn that true integrity can always be reinforced in our professional lives. Integrity is crucial in the marketplace. Many professing believers are not influencing our culture because their lives Monday through Friday are not that different from the lives of those with whom they work. The best place to engage and transform our culture is not the place where we spend Sunday morning but the place where we spend Monday through Friday of each week.

Finally, we learn that integrity will ultimately be revealed in the public life. Everything King Darius knew about God he learned by observing Daniel's public life of integrity. Think about that. We are being watched, and our world still wants to know, "Is your God able to deliver you?" They will never know unless we are men and women of integrity.

The Daniel Code

Our culture brings new challenges to our Christian faith with each passing day. New assaults on religious liberties, cherished for centuries, are happening with increasing regularity. And Daniel would be able to relate. Like many of us, Daniel grew up in a culture built on biblical truth and centered in traditional family values. And then he found himself living in a culture that was hostile to everything he had ever known. His value system, his truth claims, and his moral compass were challenged repeatedly at every turn. His world was suddenly a world of pluralistic thought. But Daniel had a different spirit about him. He was a man of integrity who not only engaged his culture head-on but actually was used by God to transform it. And—just in case we need to be reminded—Daniel's God is still our God!

Seemingly with every new court decision, our twenty-first-century culture brings new challenges to our Christian values and truth claims. Those of us who once knew a Judeo-Christian culture have suddenly found ourselves living in a culture as hostile to what we believe as Babylon was to Daniel. Our world is evolving into one of massive pluralism with an encroaching paganism attached to various belief systems. Our nation—our culture—is in great need of men and women whose integrity is rooted in their private lives, reflected in their personal lives, reinforced in the professional setting, and revealed in public. May they rise up and be counted!

So Daniel has left us his own code for engaging and influencing our culture. It is centered in our personal integrity. And if we are going to find our way through a culture that has lost its way, we can't leave home without it!

CONCLUSION

You Can Survive Culture Shock

*H*istory has a way of repeating itself across the centuries. Ideas just reappear at different times, in different ways, and with different names. The Babylon of Daniel's day is still geographically with us: we simply call it modern-day Iraq. And Persia is still with us also, but it is called Iran today. Things in those places haven't changed much. Babylon's fiery furnaces are now Iraq's use of chemical weapons against its own citizens. And Persia no longer uses a lions' den; today Iran is more focused on developing its own nuclear arsenal.

As we have journeyed through the first six chapters of Daniel, we have seen what one man of courage and conviction did to influence two entire cultures. Daniel, whom we met as a young Jewish boy in exile, engaged both a pagan Babylonian culture and a pluralistic Persian one with amazing results. He lived to see the wicked King Nebuchadnezzar of Babylon declare, "There is no other God who can deliver like this. . . . Now, I, Nebuchadnezzar praise and extol and honor the King of heaven, all of whose works are truth, and His ways justice. And those who walk in pride He is able to put down" (Daniel 3:29; 4:37). And when Persia later defeated

Babylon and broke forever that empire's supremacy, Daniel lived to hear King Darius proclaim, "I make a decree that in every dominion of my kingdom men must tremble and fear before the God of Daniel. For He is the living God and steadfast forever; His kingdom is the one which shall not be destroyed, and His dominion shall endure to the end" (6:26). These are amazing professions of faith coming from two of the most unlikely prospects one could ever, in their wildest thoughts, imagine. Daniel lives on in history, and in our hearts, as a testimony to the fact that it is possible to not simply survive in a corrupt culture, but to engage it and change it as well. Daniel's God is still alive today to help make that happen.

THE GOSPEL

Daniel's message of hope and help is the good news of God's grace. We call it "the gospel" today. It still has the power to impact lives and transform cultures. In fact, Paul referred to the gospel as the "power of God" (Romans 1:16) and chose a word from which we derive our word *dynamite* to describe it. And it is gospel power—not pickets, petitions, protests, or politics—that is our only hope today.

And, as we have also seen in Daniel, the transformation of our culture begins with you, and with me, in our private world where we meet with God. The power of the gospel does not bring about a *changed* life as much as it brings about an *exchanged* life. We confess our sin and hand over to God our old life; in exchange, He gives us one that is brand-new.

Christ comes to live in us, never to leave us, empowering us to serve Him and others. Once we are filled with the Spirit of Christ, we begin the great adventure of living for Him, and we find in Him the true purpose for which we have been created in the first place. No one else on the planet has a DNA like yours. You are valuable to God. He knows you . . . where you live . . . your e-mail address. And He loves you and truly does have a wonderful plan for your life.

In fact, this new life is God's free gift to us. The Bible says, "The wages of sin is death, but the gift of God is eternal life in Christ Jesus our Lord" (Romans 6:23). We cannot earn our salvation, and we certainly do not deserve it. God gives us a transformed and eternal life because of His love and grace, and we receive this gift only through faith in Him. We are all sinners who have fallen short of God's holy standards and can do nothing to save ourselves.

Yet God is a God of love, who loves us despite of our sins. At the same time, He is a God of justice, who must therefore punish sin. This is where Jesus steps in! He is the holy and sinless God-Man, who came into this sin-filled world to suffer God's wrath and judgment for our sin. He did that when He died on the cross.

AN INVITATION

But just knowing this good news, this gospel, is not enough. You must transfer your trust in yourself and your own human efforts, no matter how noble, to Jesus Christ. And you must believe that His death and resurrection mean God's forgiveness of your sins and your own personal salvation.

Jesus said, "Behold, I stand at the door and knock. If anyone hears My voice and opens the door, I will come in to him" (Revelation 3:20). Picture, for just a moment, an imaginary door on your heart. Jesus is knocking on that door. If you would like to receive God's free offer of eternal and abundant life, you can respond to Jesus right now. Open that door to your heart and invite Him to come in. When you do, you can stand tall on His promise to you that "whoever calls on the name of the LORD shall be saved" (Romans 10:13).

If that paragraph reflects the desire of your heart, I encourage you to pray the following in your heart right now:

> *Dear Lord Jesus, I know I have sinned. I know I do not deserve eternal life. Please forgive my sin. Thank You for taking all my sin to the cross and dying in my place, dying the very death I deserved. I trust that You are the One and only One who can save me from eternal separation from a holy God. Savior, I ask You now to be the Lord and the King of my life. I turn my face to You. I accept Your gracious gifts of forgiveness and eternal life. Thank You, Lord, for coming into my life as my Savior and my Lord. In Jesus' name I pray, amen.*

A simple prayer can never save you, but Jesus can—and He will—if this prayer expresses the desire of your heart. You can now claim the promise Jesus made to all who would choose to follow Him: "Most assuredly . . . he who believes in Me has everlasting life!" (John 6:47).

Now you are ready for the great adventure for which God created you in the first place: to know Christ and to walk with Him daily from this day forth. As you do so, His Spirit, now abiding in you, will be at work to continue transforming you, making you more like Him in character and integrity.

One more thought. You will now begin to see—as you saw in Daniel's life—that knowing Christ will be reflected in your personal world . . . reinforced in your professional world . . . and revealed in your public world . . . all for His glory.

Yes, history has a way of repeating itself. That being the case, we—like Daniel—can survive culture shock. As we now go out to engage our own culture, may we dare to be a Daniel . . . dare to stand alone . . . dare to have a purpose firm . . . and dare to make it known.

As we leave our friend Daniel, may we have this truth foremost in our mind: "The Most High rules in the kingdom of men" (Daniel 4:32). He still does. He always will! He is Lord!

Mission:Dignity

*A*ll of the author's royalties and any proceeds from *The James Code*, *The Jesus Code*, *The Joshua Code*, and now *The Daniel Code* go to the support of Mission:Dignity, a ministry of the Dallas-based GuideStone Financial Resources that enables thousands of retired ministers (and, in most cases, their widows) who are living near the poverty level to live out their days with dignity and security. Many of them spent their pastoral ministry in small churches that were unable to provide adequately for their retirement. They also lived in church-owned parsonages and, upon their vocational retirement, had to vacate them as well. Mission:Dignity is a way of letting these good and godly servants know they are not forgotten and will be cared for in their declining years.

All of the expenses of this ministry are paid out of an endowment that has been raised for such, so everyone who gives to Mission:Dignity can be assured that every cent of their gift goes to one of these precious saints in need.

For additional information regarding this ministry, please go to www.guidestone.org and click on the Mission:Dignity icon, or call toll-free at 1–888–98-GUIDE (1–888–984-8433).

OTHER BOOKS BY O. S. HAWKINS

When Revival Comes
(with Jack R. Taylor)

After Revival Comes

Clues to a Successful Life

Where Angels Fear to Tread

*Tracing the Rainbow
Through the Rain*

Revive Us Again

Unmasked!

*Jonah: Meeting the God
of the Second Chance*

In Sheep's Clothing

*Tearing Down Walls and
Building Bridges*

*Moral Earthquakes and
Secret Faults*

*Rebuilding: It's Never Too Late
for a New Beginning*

*Money Talks: But What
Is It Really Saying?*

*Shields of Brass or
Shields of Gold?*

Good News for Great Days

Drawing the Net

Culture Shock

High Calling, High Anxiety

The Question for Our Time

The Art of Connecting

*GuideStones: Ancient
Landmarks*

The Pastor's Primer

More Good News for Great Days

Getting Down to Brass Tacks

Antology

*The Pastor's Guide to Leading
and Living*

About the Author

For more than twenty-five years, O. S. Hawkins served pastorates including the First Baptist Church in Fort Lauderdale, Florida, and the First Baptist Church in Dallas, Texas. A native of Fort Worth, he has three earned degrees (BBA, MDiv, and DMin) as well as several honorary degrees. He is president of GuideStone Financial Resources, which serves 250,000 pastors, church staff members, missionaries, doctors, nurses, university professors, and other workers in various Christian organizations with their retirement and benefit service needs. He is the author of more than thirty books, including the bestselling *The Joshua Code*, *The Jesus Code*, and *The James Code*, and preaches regularly at conferences, universities, business groups, and churches across the nation. He and his wife, Susie, have two married daughters and six grandchildren.

Follow O. S. Hawkins on Twitter @oshawkins.
Visit www.oshawkins.com for free resources.

CHALLENGE YOUR

faith

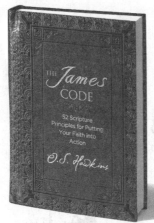

Make Your MARK

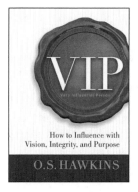

VIP takes readers through what it takes to create a life of Vision, Influence, and Purpose. Through inspirational stories, biblical examples, and charged challenges toward greatness, *VIP* illuminates a path for you to uncover what it is going to take for you to become a VIP, a Very Influential Person.

One hundred percent of the author's royalties and proceeds go to support Mission:Dignity—a ministry providing support for impoverished retired pastors and missionaries.